MASTER YOUR EMOTIONS

A PRACTICAL GUIDE TO OVERCOME
NEGATIVITY AND BETTER MANAGE YOUR
FEELINGS

THIBAUT MEURISSE

Edited by
KERRY J DONOVAN

CONTENTS

WHY THIS BOOK

Many books discuss emotions and how they affect your life, but they rarely provide a comprehensive view of what emotions are, where they come from, what their role is, or how they affect your life.

Emotions are among the trickiest things to deal with and, unfortunately, too often, you and I will fall prey to their mystical power. We find ourselves unable to break their spell. Because emotions determine the quality of our lives and affect every aspect of it, our inability to understand how emotions work can prevent us from designing our ideal life and from fulfilling our potential.

If you struggle to deal with negative emotions or want to learn how emotions work and how you can use them as a tool for your personal growth, this book is for you.

By the end of this book, you will know how emotions work and, more importantly, you will be better equipped to deal with them.

INTRODUCTION

> " The mind is its own place, and in itself can make a
> heaven of Hell, a hell of Heaven.

— John Milton, poet.

We all experience a wide range of emotions throughout our lives. I had to admit, while writing this book, I experienced highs and lows myself. At first, I was filled with excitement and thrilled at the idea of providing people with a guide to help them understand their emotions. I imagined how readers' lives would improve as they learned to control their emotions. My motivation was high and I couldn't help but imagine how great the book would be.

Or so I thought.

After the initial excitement, the time came to sit down to write the actual book, and that's when the excitement wore off pretty quickly. Suddenly ideas that looked great in my mind felt dull. My writing seemed boring, and I felt as though I had nothing substantive or valuable to contribute.

Sitting at my desk and writing became more challenging each day. I started losing confidence. Who was I to write a book about emotions if I couldn't even master my own emotions? How ironic! I considered giving up. There are already plenty of books on the topic, so why add one more?

At the same time, I realized this book was a perfect opportunity to work on my emotional issues. And who doesn't suffer from negative emotions from time to time? We all have highs and lows, don't we? The key is what we *do* with our lows. Are we using our emotions to grow and learn or are we beating ourselves up over them?

So, let's talk about *your* emotions now. Let me start by asking you this:

How do you feel right now?

Knowing how you feel is the first step toward taking control of your emotions. You may have spent so much time internalizing you've lost touch with your feelings. Perhaps you answered as follows: "I feel this book could be useful," or "I really feel I could learn something from this book."

However, none of these answers reflect on how you feel. You don't 'feel like this,' or 'feel like that,' you simply 'feel.' You don't 'feel like' this book could be useful, you 'think' this book could be useful, and that generates an emotion which makes you 'feel' excited about reading it. Feelings manifest as physical sensations in your body, not as an idea in your mind. Perhaps, the reason the word 'feel' is so often overused or misused is because we don't want to talk about our emotions.

So, how do you feel now?

Why is it important to talk about emotions?

How you feel determines the quality of your life. Your emotions can make your life miserable or truly magical. That's why they are among the most essential things on which to focus. Your emotions color all your experiences. When you feel good, everything seems, feels, or tastes better. You also think better thoughts. Your energy levels are higher and possibilities seem limitless. Conversely, when you feel depressed, everything seems dull. You have little energy and you become unmotivated. You feel stuck in a place (mentally and physically) you don't want to be, and the future looks gloomy.

Your emotions can also act as a powerful guide. They can tell you something is wrong and allow you to make changes in your life. As such, they may be among the most powerful personal growth tools you have.

Sadly, neither your teachers nor your parents taught you how emotions work or how to control them. I find it ironic that just about anything comes with a how-to manual, while your mind doesn't. You've never received an instruction manual to teach you how your mind works and how to use it to better manage your emotions, have you? I haven't. In fact, until now, I doubt one even existed.

What you'll learn in this book

This book is the how-to manual your parents should have given you at birth. It's the instruction manual you should have received at school. In it, I'll share everything you need to know about emotions so you can overcome your fears and limitations and become the type of person you want to be.

More specifically, this book will help you:

- Understand what emotions are and how they impact your life
- Understand how emotions form and how you can use them for your personal growth
- Identify negative emotions that control your life and learn to overcome them
- Change your story to take better control over your life and create a more compelling future,
- Reprogram your mind to experience more positive emotions.
- Deal with negative emotions and condition your mind to create more positive ones
- Gain all the tools you need to start recognizing and controlling your emotions

Here is a more detailed summary of what you'll learn in this book:

In **Part I**, we'll discuss what emotions are. You'll learn why your brain is wired to focus on negativity and what you can do to counter this effect. You'll also discover how your beliefs impinge upon your emotions. Finally, you'll learn how negative emotions work and why they are so tricky.

In **Part II**, we'll go over the things that directly impact your emotions. You'll understand the roles your body, your thoughts, your words, or your sleep, play in your life and how you can use them to change your emotions.

In **Part III**, you'll learn how emotions form and how to condition your mind to experience more positive emotions.

And finally, in **Part IV**, we'll discuss how to use your emotions as a tool for personal growth. You'll learn why you experience emotions such as fear or depression and how they work.

Let's get started.

HOW TO USE THIS BOOK

I encourage you to read through this book at least once. After that, I invite you to revisit the book and focus on the section(s) you want to explore in more depth.

In this book, I include several different exercises. Though I don't expect you to go through them all, my hope is you'll pick some and apply them in your life. Remember, the results you'll get out of this book depend on how much time and effort you're willing to put in.

If you feel this book could be of any use to your family members or friends, make sure to share it with them. Emotions are complicated and I believe it would benefit us all to deepen our understanding of the topic.

Want to master your motivation too?

Master Your Emotions is the first book in the "**Mastery Series**"

You can get the second book, *Master Your Motivation* at the URL below:

http://mybook.to/master_motivation

"In a modern world swamped with information overload, this book is a "best friend" guide to getting you going again whether in business, at home or with life in general."

— AMAZON REVIEWER

Your Free Step-By-Step Workbook

To help you master your emotions I've created a workbook as a companion guide to his book. I highly encourage you to download it at the following URL:

http://whatispersonaldevelopment.org/mye-workbook

I'll also send you a free eBook. It will help you tremendously on your personal development journey.

If you have any difficulties downloading the workbook contact me at:

thibaut.meurisse@gmail.com

and I will send it to you as soon as possible.

Alternatively, you can also use the workbook available at the end of this book. If you want to get a physical version of the workbook go to the URL below:

http://mybook.to/MYE_workbook

PART I

WHAT EMOTIONS ARE

Have you ever wondered what emotions are and what purpose they serve?

In this section, we'll discuss how your survival mechanism affects your emotions. Then, we'll explain what the 'ego' is and how it impacts your emotions. Finally, we'll discover the mechanism behind emotions and learn why it can be so hard to deal with negative ones.

1
_____

HOW YOUR SURVIVAL MECHANISM
AFFECTS YOUR EMOTIONS

Why people have a bias towards negativity

Your brain is designed for survival, which explains why you're able to read this book at this very moment. When you think about it, the probability of you being born was extremely low. For this miracle to happen, all the generations before you had to survive long enough to procreate. In their quest for survival and procreation, they must have faced death hundreds or perhaps thousands of times.

Fortunately, unlike your ancestors, you're (probably) not facing death every day. In fact, in many parts of the world, life has never been safer. Yet, your survival mechanism hasn't changed much. Your brain still scans your environment looking for potential threats.

In many ways, some parts of your brain have become obsolete. While you may not be seconds away from being eaten by a predator, your brain still gives significantly more weight to adverse events than to positive ones.

Fear of rejection is one example of a bias toward negativity. In the past, being rejected by your tribe would reduce your chances of survival significantly. Therefore, you learned to look for any sign of rejection, and this became hardwired in your brain.

Nowadays, being rejected often carries little or no consequence to your long-term survival. You can be hated by the entire world and still have a job, a roof and plenty of food on the table, yet, your brain remains programmed to perceive rejection as a threat to your survival.

This hardwiring is why rejection can be so painful. While you know most rejections are no big deal, you nevertheless feel the emotional pain. If you listen to your mind, you may even create a whole drama around it. You may believe you aren't worthy of love and dwell on a rejection for days or weeks. Worse still, you may become depressed as a result of this rejection.

One single criticism can often outweigh hundreds of positive ones. That's why, an author with fifty 5-star reviews, is likely to feel terrible when they receive a single 1-star review. While the author understands the 1-star review isn't a threat to her survival, her authorial brain doesn't. It likely interprets the negative review as a threat to her ego which triggers an emotional reaction.

The fear of rejection can also lead you to over-dramatize events. If your boss criticized you at work, your brain might see the criticism as a threat and you now think, "What if my boss fires me? What if I can't find a job quickly enough and my wife leaves me? What about my kids? What if I can't see them again?"

While you are fortunate to have such a useful survival mechanism, it is also your responsibility to separate real threats from imaginary ones. If you don't, you'll experience unnecessary pain and worry that will negatively impact the quality of your life. To overcome this bias towards negativity, you must reprogram your mind. One of a human being's greatest powers is our ability to use our thoughts to shape our reality and interpret events in a more empowering way. This book will teach you how to do this.

* * *

Action Step

Complete the corresponding exercise in the workbook (*Section I. What Emotions are - 1. Bias towards negativity*).

* * *

Why your brain's job isn't to make you happy

Your brain's primary responsibility is not to make you happy, but to ensure your survival. Thus, if you want to be happy, you must actively take control of your emotions rather than hoping you'll be happy because it's your natural state. In the following section, we'll discuss what happiness is and how it works.

How dopamine can mess with your happiness

Dopamine is a neurotransmitter that, among other functions, plays a significant role in rewarding certain behaviors. When dopamine releases into specific areas of your brain—the pleasure centers—you get an intense sense of wellbeing similar to a high. This sense of wellbeing is what happens during exercise, when you gamble, have sex, or eat great food.

One of the roles of dopamine is to ensure you look for food so you don't die of starvation, and you search for a mate so you can reproduce. Without dopamine, our species would likely be extinct by now. It's a pretty good thing, right?

Well, yes and no. In today's world, this reward system is, in many cases, obsolete. In the past, dopamine directly linked to our survival, now, it can be stimulated artificially. A great example of this effect is social media, which uses psychology to suck as much time as possible out of your life. Have you noticed all these notifications that pop up regularly? They're used to trigger a release of dopamine so you stay connected, and the longer you stay connected, the more money the services make. Watching pornography or gambling also leads to a release of dopamine which can make these activities highly addictive.

Fortunately, we don't need to act each time our brain releases dopamine. For instance, we don't need to continuously check our Facebook newsfeeds just because it gives us a pleasurable shot of dopamine.

Today's society is selling a version of happiness that can make us *un*happy. We've become addicted to dopamine mainly because of marketers who have found effective ways to exploit our brains. We receive multiple shots of dopamine throughout the day and we love it. But is that the same thing as happiness?

Worse than that, dopamine can create real addictions with severe consequences on our health. Research conducted at Tulane University showed that, when permitted to self-stimulate their pleasure center, participants did it an average of forty times per minute. They chose the stimulation of their pleasure center over food, even refusing to eat when hungry!

Korean, Lee Seung Seop is an extreme case of this syndrome. In 2005, Mr Seop died after playing a video game for fifty-eight hours straight with very little food or water, and no sleep. The subsequent investigation concluded the cause of death was heart failure induced by exhaustion and dehydration. He was only twenty-eight years old.

To take control of your emotions, you must understand the role dopamine plays and how it affects your happiness. Are you addicted to your phone? Are you glued to your TV? Or maybe you spend too much time playing video games. Most of us are addicted to something. For some people it's obvious, but for others, it's more subtle. For instance, you could be addicted to thinking. To better control your emotions, you must recognize and shed the light on your addictions as they can rob you of your happiness.

The 'one day I will' myth

Do you believe that one day you will achieve your dream and finally be happy? It is unlikely to happen. You may (and I hope you will) achieve your goal, but you won't live 'happily ever after.' This thinking is just another trick your mind plays on you.

Your mind quickly acclimates to new situations, which is probably the result of evolution and our need to adapt continually to survive and reproduce. This acclimatization is also probably why the new car or house you want will only make you happy for a while. Once the initial excitement wears off, you'll move on to crave the next exciting thing. This phenomenon is known as 'hedonic adaptation.'

How hedonic adaptation works

Let me share an interesting study that will likely change the way you see happiness. This study, which was conducted in 1978 on lottery winners and paraplegics, was incredibly eye-opening for me. The investigation evaluated how winning the lottery or becoming a paraplegic influence happiness:

The study found that one year after the event, both groups were just as happy as they were beforehand. Yes, just as happy (or unhappy). You can find more about it by watching Dan Gilbert's TED Talk, The Surprising Science of Happiness.

Perhaps you believe that you'll be happy once you've 'made it.' But, as the above study on happiness shows, this is simply not true. No matter what happens to you, your mind works by reverting to your predetermined level of happiness once you've adapted to the new event.

Does that mean you can't be happier than you are right now? No. What it means is that, in the long run, external events have minimal impact on your level of happiness.

In fact, according to Sonja Lyubomirsky, author of *The How of Happiness*, fifty percent of our happiness is determined by genetics, forty percent by internal factors, and only ten percent by external factors. These external factors include such things as whether we're single or married, rich or poor, and similar social influences.

The influence of external factors is probably way less than you thought. The bottom line is this: Your attitude towards life influences your happiness, not what happens to you.

By now, you understand how your survival mechanism negatively impacts your emotions and prevents you from experiencing more joy and happiness in your life. In the next section, we'll learn about the ego.

* * *

Action step

Use the workbook to write down things that give you 'shots of dopamine' (*Section I. What Emotions are - 2. Happiness*)

2

WHAT IS THE EGO

Your survival mechanism is not the only factor affecting your emotions. Your ego also plays a significant role in shaping the way you feel. Thus, to gain more control over your emotions, it is fundamental you understand what your ego is and how it works.

Now, let's clarify what we mean by ego. We often say of someone that, "he has a *big ego*," referring to the ego as something close to pride. While pride is undoubtedly a *manifestation* of ego, that's only one part of it. You may show no pride and appear humble while still being controlled by your ego.

So, what is the ego?

The ego refers to the self-identity you've constructed throughout your life. How was this identity created? Put simply, the ego was created through your thoughts and, as a mind-created identity, has no concrete reality.

Events that happen to you bear no meaning in themselves. You give them meaning only through your interpretation of those events. Additionally, you accept things about yourself because people told you to do so. What's more, you identify with your name, your age, your religion, your political belief, or your occupation in a similar way.

This attachment has consequences. As we'll see later in this book, attachment creates beliefs, and these beliefs lead you to experience certain emotions. For instance, you may become offended when people criticize your religion or attack your political principles.

Note that throughout this book, we'll refer to the ego as your 'story' or your 'identity' using these words interchangeably.

Are you aware of your ego?

Your understanding of the way your ego works depends on your level of self-awareness. People at the lowest level of consciousness are not even aware the ego exists and, as a result, are enslaved by it.

On the other hand, highly self-conscious people can see through their ego. They understand how belief works and how excessive attachment to a set of beliefs can create suffering in their life. In effect, these individuals become the master of their mind and are at peace with themselves.

Note that the ego is neither good nor bad; it's just a result of a lack of self-awareness. It fades away as you become aware of it since ego and awareness cannot coexist.

Your ego's need for an identity

Your ego is a selfish entity, only concerned about its survival. Interestingly, it's somewhat similar to your brain in the way it operates. It has its survival mechanism and will do whatever it can to persist. As with your brain, its primary concern is neither your happiness nor your peace of mind. On the contrary, your ego is restless. It wants you to be a go-getter. It wants you to do, acquire and achieve great things so you can become a 'somebody.'

As we already mentioned, your ego needs an identity to exist. The way it does that is through identification with things, people, or beliefs and ideas.

Now, let's look at some of the things your ego uses to strengthen its identity:

Physical items

The ego likes to identify with material things. It thrives in today's world. Perhaps, we can say capitalism and the consumer society we're living in today is the creation of collective egos, which is why it has been the dominant economic model in recent decades.

Marketers correctly understand people's need to identify with things. They know people don't just buy a product, they also purchase the emotions or story attached to the product. Often, you acquire certain clothes or a particular car because you want to tell a story about yourself. For instance, you may want to enhance your status, look cool or express your unique personality, and choose the products most closely associated with these ideals.

Using things to create a story you can identify with is how the ego works. It doesn't mean things are wrong, *per se*. It's a negative issue only when you become overly attached to material things, believing they can fulfill you—which they can't.

Your body

Most people derive their self-worth from their physical appearance. Your ego loves the way you look because it is the easiest thing to recognize and quantify. When you strongly associate with your physical appearance, you tend to identify more easily with physical and emotional pain. Believe it or not, you can observe your body without 'identifying with' it.

Friends/acquaintances

The ego also derives its sense of identity from your relationships with others. The ego is only interested in what it can get from them. In other words, the ego thrives on the way it can use people to strengthen its identity.

If you are honest with yourself, you'll realize most of the things you do attempt to obtain the approval of others. You want your parents to be proud of you, your boss to respect you, and your wife to love you.

Now, let's see in more detail how the ego works in the following cases:

Parent/child relationships

Some parents' egos lead to the creation of a strong sense of attachment and identification with their children. This attachment is based on the false belief their children are their 'possessions.' As a result, they try to control their childrens' lives and 'use' them to live the life *they* wanted to live when they were younger—this is called living vicariously through your children. You see this all the time. Next time you watch a junior soccer (or baseball) game, watch the parents on the touchline to see how some react. Try spotting the parents living vicariously—they are the ones screaming the loudest, and not merely in encouragement. This may happen mostly unconsciously.

Couples

The feeling of needing someone is very much a play of the ego as well. Anthony de Mello has a beautiful way to put it when he says:

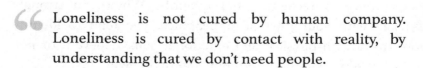 Loneliness is not cured by human company. Loneliness is cured by contact with reality, by understanding that we don't need people.

Once you realize you don't actually *need* anyone, you can start enjoying people's company. You can see them as they really are rather than trying to get something from them.

Your beliefs

Your ego also uses beliefs to strengthen its identity. In extreme cases, people become so attached to their beliefs they are ready to die to protect them. Worse still, they are willing to kill people who disagree with them. Religion is a perfect illustration of the dangers of excessive attachment to beliefs. The ego will use *any belief* to strengthen its identity, whether these beliefs are religious, political, or metaphysical.

Other objects of identification

Now let's have a look at a (non-exhaustive) list of things your ego generally derives its identity from:

- Your body
- Your name
- Your gender
- Your nationality
- Your culture
- Your family/friends
- Your beliefs (political beliefs, religious, etc.)
- Your personal story (your interpretation of the past, your expectations regarding the future)
- Your problems (illnesses, financial situation, victim mindset, etc.)
- Your age
- Your job
- Your social status

- Your role (as employee, homemaker, parental status, employment status, etc.)
- Material items (your house, car, clothes, phone, etc.)
- Your desires

The ego's main characteristics

Here are some main aspects of the ego:

- The ego tends to equate 'having' with 'being,' which is why the ego likes to identify with objects.
- The ego lives through comparison. Your ego likes to compare itself with other egos.
- The ego is never satisfied. Your ego always wants more. More fame, more stuff, more recognition, and so on.
- The ego's sense of self-worth often depends on the worth you have in the eyes of others. Your ego needs the approval of other people to feel valued.

The ego's need to feel superior

Your ego wants to feel superior to other egos. It wants to stand out and needs to create artificial separations to do that. Here are some strategies it employs:

- **Enhancing its value through people.** If you have smart/famous friends, your ego will associate with them to strengthen its identity. This is why some people love to tell others how smart, rich or famous their friends are.
- **Gossiping.** People gossip because it makes them feel different and superior in some way. This is why some people like to put other people down and talk behind their back; it makes them—and everybody else in their gossiping group—feel superior.

- **Manifesting an inferiority complex.** This hides a desire to be better than others. Yes, even in this case, people want to feel superior.
- **Exhibiting a superiority complex.** This hides the fear of not being good enough.
- **Looking for fame.** This offers the illusion of superiority, which is why people often dream of becoming famous.
- **Being right.** The ego loves to be correct. It's an excellent way for it to affirm its existence. Have you noticed that everybody, from Adolf Hitler to Nelson Mandela, believe they're doing the right thing? Most people think they are correct. But can everybody be right?
- **Complaining.** When people complain, by definition they believe they are right and others are wrong. It works with objects as well. Have you ever bumped into a table and complained or even insulted it? I have, and the darned table was wrong to be in my way, wasn't it?
- **Seeking attention.** The ego likes to stand out. It loves recognition, praise or admiration. To seek attention, people may also commit crimes, wear eccentric clothes, or have tattoos all over their bodies.

Your ego's impact on your emotion

Understanding the way your ego works can help you better control your emotions. To do this, you must first realize your current story is the result of a strong identification with people, things or ideas. This intense identification is the root of many of the negative emotions you experience in your life. For instance:

- When life doesn't unfold according to your personal story you get upset, or
- When someone challenges one of your beliefs you become defensive.

In short, most of your emotions are based on your personal story and the way you perceive the world. As you replace your current story with a more empowering one—while, at the same time, letting go of your excessive attachment to things, people or ideas —you will be able to experience more positive emotions. Later in this book, we'll see how you can change the way you interpret events.

* * *

Action step

Take a few minutes to answer the questions in the workbook (*Section I. What Emotions are - 3. The nature of the ego*).

3

THE NATURE OF EMOTIONS

Emotions can be tricky. In this section, we'll discuss in depth how they work. By understanding the mechanism behind emotions, you'll be able to manage them more effectively as they arise.

The first thing to understand is that emotions come and go. One moment you feel happy, the next you feel sad. While you do have some control over your emotions, you must also recognize their unpredictable nature. If you expect to be happy all the time, you set yourself up for failure. You then risk blaming yourself when you 'fail' to be happy, or even worse, beat yourself up for it.

To start taking control of your emotions you must accept they are transient. You must learn to let them pass without feeling the need to identify strongly with them. You must allow yourself to feel sad without adding commentaries such as, "I shouldn't be sad," or "What's wrong with me?" Instead, you must allow reality to just be.

No matter how mentally tough you are, you'll still experience sadness, grief or depression in your life—hopefully not at the same time, and not continually. At times you'll feel disappointed, betrayed, insecure, resentful or ashamed. You'll doubt yourself and doubt your ability to be the person you want to be. But that's okay because emotions come, but, more importantly, they go.

Your negative emotions are not bad or useless.

You may blame yourself for experiencing negative emotions or, perhaps, you see yourself as mentally weak. You may even believe something is wrong with you. However, despite what your inner voice may say, your emotions aren't bad. Emotions are simply emotions. Nothing more.

As such, being depressed doesn't make you less of a person than you were three weeks ago when you were happy. Feeling sad now doesn't mean you'll never be able to laugh again.

Remember this: the way you interpret emotions, as well as the blame game you engage in, creates suffering, not the emotions themselves.

Negative emotions can actually be helpful. Sometimes, you need to touch rock-bottom before you can reach the top. Even the toughest people on earth become depressed. Elon Musk never imagined he would have a mental breakdown, but he did and he bounced back. After losing his fiancée, Abraham Lincoln was depressed for months. This tragic event didn't prevent him from becoming president of the United States. Negative emotions often serve a purpose. They may serve as a wake-up call. They may help you learn something positive about yourself. Of course, when you're under their spell, it may be difficult to look at the bright side of things, but in hindsight, you may realize emotions—even sad ones—had their role to play in your ultimate success.

The positive role of negative emotions

Your emotions are not here to make your life harder, but to tell you something. Without them, you wouldn't grow.

Think of your negative emotions as the emotional equivalent of physical pain. While you hate being in pain, if you didn't have pain, chances are you would be dead by now. Physical pain sends a powerful signal that something is wrong, nudging you to take action of some kind. It could be to consult your doctor, which may lead you to undergo surgery, change your diet, or increase exercise. Without physical pain, you wouldn't do any of these things and your situation would worsen, potentially leading to a premature death.

Emotions work the same way. They signal you to do something about your current situation. Perhaps, you need to let go of some people, quit your job, or remove a disempowering story that creates suffering in your life.

The fleeting nature of emotions

No matter how depressed you are, how much grief you're experiencing, or how horrible you feel at a given point in time, this shall pass.

Look at some of the negative emotions you experienced in the past. Remember the worse times in your life. During these most difficult periods, you were probably so caught up in your emotions you imagined never being able to escape them. You couldn't imagine being happy again. But even these episodes ended. Eventually, the clouds dissipated and the real you shone again.

Your emotions come and they go. Your depression *will* go, your sadness *will* vanish and your anger *will* fade away.

Bear in mind, if you experience the same emotions repeatedly, it probably means you hold disempowering beliefs and need to change something in your life. We'll discuss how later.

If you suffer from severe, chronic depression, it might be a good idea to consult a specialist.

The trickiness of emotions

Have you ever felt you'll never be happy again? Have you ever been so attached to your emotions you thought they'll never go away?

Don't worry, it's a common feeling.

Negative emotions act as a filter that taints the quality of your experiences. During a negative episode, every experience is perceived through this filter. While the world outside may remain the same, you will experience it in a completely different way based on how you feel.

For instance, when you're depressed, you don't enjoy the food you eat, the movie you see, or the activities in which you engage. You only see the negative side of things, feeling trapped and powerless. On the other hand, when you're in a positive mood, everything in life appears better. Food tastes great, you enjoy all the activities you partake in, you're naturally friendlier.

You may now believe that, armed with the knowledge you have gained from this book, you'll never be depressed again. Wrong! You'll keep experiencing sadness, frustration, depression, or resentment, but hopefully, each time these occur, you'll become wiser and wiser, remembering that *this too, shall pass.*

I have to admit; I can easily be fooled by my emotions. While I know I am not my emotions, I still give them too much credit and fail to realize they are just temporary visitors. More importantly, I fail to remember they are *not* me. Emotions always come and go, but I remain. Once the emotional storm has passed, I generally feel like an idiot for having taken my feelings so seriously. Do you?

Interestingly, external factors might not be—and often aren't—the direct cause of a sudden change in your emotional state. You can be in the same situation, with the same job, the same amount of money in your bank account, and have the same problems as always, but experience radically different emotional states. In fact, if you look at your past, this is often what happens. You are mildly depressed for a couple of hours or a few days, before bouncing back to your 'default' emotional state. During this period of emotional stress, your environment doesn't change at all. The only thing that changes is your internal dialogue.

I encourage you to make a conscious effort to notice whenever such events happen and start seeing through your emotions' trickery. You might want to go one step further and record these events in a journal. By doing so, you will gain a deeper understanding of how emotions work and, as a result, you will be better equipped to manage them.

The evil power of emotions

> An emotion usually represents an amplified energized thought pattern, and because of its often-overpowering energetic charges, it is not easy initially to stay present enough to be able to watch it. It wants to take you over, and it usually succeeds—unless there is enough presence in you.
>
> — ECKHART TOLLE, THE POWER OF NOW.

Negative emotions are like a spell. While you're under their influence, breaking free from them seems impossible. You may know dwelling on the same thoughts is pointless, yet you can't help but go along with the flow. Feeling an intense pull, you keep identifying with your thoughts and, as a result, feel worse and worse. When this happens, no rational argument seems to work.

The more these emotions fit your personal story, the stronger the pull becomes. For instance, if you believe you aren't good enough, you may experience negative emotions such as guilt or shame each time you judge what you do is 'not good enough.' Because you've experienced these emotions so many times before, they have become an automatic response.

For more information on how the identification with emotions works, refer to the section "Identification."

The filtering power of emotions

Your emotional state can drastically affect your outlook on life, leading you to act and behave differently.

When you're in a positive state, you have more energy available. This energy gives you:

- More confidence in everything you do
- An openness to consider new actions that could improve your life
- The ability to leave or break out of your comfort zone
- More emotional room to persevere during tough times
- Better ideas and enhanced creativity, and
- Easy access to positive emotions within the same emotional range.

When you're in a negative state of mind, you have less energy available, giving you:

- A lack of confidence that affects everything you do

- A lack of motivation that reduces the scope of actions you're willing to take
- A reluctance to take on new challenges and leave your comfort zone
- A reduced ability to persevere in the face of setbacks, and
- A propensity to attract negative thoughts within the same emotional range.

Let me share with you a real example from my own life. Both cases happened under the same external conditions. The only difference was my emotional state at the time.

Case 1 - Feeling excited about my online business:

- More confidence in everything I do: I feel as though my ideas are good. I'm excited to work on my books and eager to write articles. I am open to sharing my work and promoting it.
- An openness to consider new courses of action: I am open to new ideas or to work on a new project. I can think of ways to collaborate with other authors and start building a new coaching program to offer my audience.
- The ability to get out of my comfort zone: It becomes easier for me to push myself beyond my comfort zone. I may contact people I don't know, or run 'Facebook Lives' for instance.
- More emotional room to persevere: I stick to my projects even when I lack motivation.
- Better ideas and enhanced creativity: I am open to new ideas. I might come up with new ideas for books, articles or other creative projects.
- Easy access to more positive emotions: I attract more positive emotions. At the same time, my mind rejects negative thoughts more efficiently by refusing to identify with them.

Case 2 - Feeling mildly depressed due to my lack of results:

- A lack of confidence: I start doubting myself and all the projects I'm currently working on. Suddenly, everything I do becomes useless or 'not good enough.' Thoughts like, "What's the point?", "I'm not going to make it," or "I'm stupid," cross my mind. Promoting myself becomes a significant challenge.
- A lack of motivation: I don't feel like doing anything. I'm attacked by, and am unable to escape, negative thoughts. I have the same negative thoughts again and again, which repeat like a broken record. They seem so real and taint all my experiences.
- Difficulty taking on new challenges: I have little energy left over to leave my comfort and undertake challenging projects.
- A reduced ability to persevere: I have difficulty finishing tasks and I procrastinate over tasks I 'should' be working on.
- A propensity to attract negative thoughts: I invite more and more negative thoughts. Although these thoughts may have been crossing my mind before, now they stick fast. By identifying with these thoughts, I generate more negative emotions.

Both cases happened only a few days apart. The external environment was the same, but my emotional state was radically different and led me to take different actions.

The magnetic power of emotions

Your emotions act like magnets. They attract thoughts on the same 'wave.' That's why, when you're in a negative state, you easily attract other negative thoughts, and by latching onto these thoughts you make the situation worse.

As Eckhart Tolle wrote in *The Power of Now:*

> Often, a vicious circle builds up between your thinking and the emotion: they feed each other. The thought pattern creates a magnified reflection of itself in the form of an emotion, and the vibrational frequency of the emotion keeps feeding the original thought pattern.

— ECKHART TOLLE

Now, let's see what you can do to break free from that magnetic power

Breaking the magnetic power of emotions

Let's say you have a bad day at work and you're in a terrible mood. The negative state you're in causes you to attract more negative thoughts. Suddenly, you fixate on the fact you're still single at thirty and start beating yourself up over it. Then, you blame yourself for being overweight. You also remember you have to go to the office the following Saturday which reminds you how much your job sucks.

Do you see how much easier it is to attract negative thoughts when you're feeling low? To prevent this from happening, must remove the habit of clustering negative thoughts together.

Real-life example:

I have knee problems, which prevents me from practicing many sports. Since I've always loved sports, these injuries have been a source of emotional pain. Fortunately, I seldom feel pain in my knees, but when I do, it can trigger negative emotions. One day, as

I was observing my thought process, I realized experiencing pain in my knees negatively affected my mood, triggering more negative emotions in a negative feedback loop. The pain would cause me to focus on all the things that were going wrong, from my work to my personal life. As a result, I would experience negative emotions for hours, or even days.

The point I'm making is, no matter how great your life is, if you spend most of your time focusing on your problems, you'll become depressed. Thus, to reduce negative emotions, you must learn to compartmentalize your issues. Don't let your mind over-dramatize things by clustering unrelated matters. It will only make you feel worse. Instead, remember that negative emotions exist only in your mind. Taken separately, most of your issues aren't such a big deal, and no rule that says you have to solve them all at once.

Start noticing how you feel. Record your negative emotions. Look at what triggers them. The more you do this, the more you will uncover specific patterns. For example, let's say you felt sad for a couple of days, ask yourself the following questions:

- What triggered my emotions?
- What fueled them over the two days?
- What story was I telling myself?
- How and why did I get out of my slump?
- What can I learn from this episode?

Answering these questions will be invaluable and will vastly help you deal with similar issues in the future.

Your emotional accessibility

We previously saw you attract thoughts that matched your emotional state. The opposite is also true. You can't attract thoughts that are out of sync with how you feel at any given time. Even if you tried to think positive thoughts, your mind wouldn't be receptive to them. This is why during periods of sadness, while positive thoughts may cross your mind from time to time, you won't be able to associate with them and you won't be able to change your emotional state.

Your emotional set point

Have you ever been told to cheer up when you were grieving, or express gratitude when you were depressed? Did it help? It probably didn't. This is because the emotional state you were in didn't allow you access to these emotions.

In their book, *Ask and It is Given,* Ester and Jerry Hicks offer a model to explain how emotional ranges are connected and how we can move up the ladder from negative, to more positive emotions. For instance, in this model, depression or hopelessness is at the bottom of the ladder followed by anger. What it means is that when you feel depressed, signs of anger indicate you're climbing the emotional ladder. This makes sense. When you're angry you have more energy than when you're depressed, right?

Recently, after being depressed for a while, I experienced feelings of anger. For some reason, I got tired of the stories and excuses running through my mind, and I used the anger as a fuel to complete the tasks I had been avoiding. As a result, I was able to create momentum and climb the emotional ladder.

Whenever you experience negative emotions, watch for emotions that give you more energy. So-called negative emotions like anger can help you overcome even more disempowering emotions, like hopelessness. Only *you* know how you feel. Therefore, if anger feels better, accept it.

Emotions and mental suffering

Did you know you create a lot of unnecessary pain in your life? Each time you lock on to a thought, or hold onto an emotion, you suffer. A great example of this is how you react to physical pain. Whenever you feel pain, your first reaction is to interpret it. When you do so, you generate negative thoughts. Your identification with these thoughts is what creates mental suffering. Below are some of the ideas that may cross your mind in these situations:

- What if this pain never goes away?
- What if I can't do X, Y, Z anymore because of the pain?
- What if it gets worse?
- What if I need to undergo surgery?
- What if I can't go to work? I have an important project I must finish on time
- With this pain, today's going to be challenging
- I don't have money. How will I pay hospital bills if things get worse?

This internal dialogue creates suffering but does nothing to help solve the problem. You can still function properly and take appropriate actions without dwelling on any of the above worries. Negative emotions are not the problem, the mental suffering you create out of these emotions is.

Another example of mental suffering is procrastination. Have you ever delayed starting a task for days or weeks just to realize it wasn't a big deal once you'd completed it? I have. What was the most exhausting part, the task itself, or the time you spent worrying about it?

Or perhaps you didn't sleep long enough and keep telling yourself today's going to be a rough day. As you imagine all the tasks you need to do, you already feel exhausted.

Psychologists have shown that mental suffering is what consumes most of your energy. After all, sitting at a desk all day shouldn't be that tiring, yet many of us feel exhausted at the end of the day. In his classic book, *How to Stop Worrying and Start Living*, Dale Carnegie wrote the following:

> One of America's most distinguished psychiatrists, Dr. A. A. Brill, goes even further. He declares, "One hundred percent of the fatigue of the sedentary worker in good health is due to psychological factors, by which we mean emotional factors.
>
> — DALE CARNEGIE

People inflict a tremendous amount of suffering on themselves. As you continue reading this book, you'll realize the idiocy of this activity. You'll notice people around you dwelling on a past they cannot alter. You'll see your family members and friends worrying about a future they cannot predict. You'll witness people having the same repeated thoughts, running in circles to fight a problem that exists only in their mind. For thousands of years, mystics have told us that problems are in our mind. They have repeatedly invited us to look within. Yet, today, how many people are listening?

Too many of us are addicted to our problems. Instead of letting go, we complain, we play the victim, we blame other people, or we discuss our issues without doing anything to solve them. To reduce this mental suffering, we must refuse to interpret our emotions in a negative and disempowering way.

Why problems don't exist

If we go one step further and objectively look at reality, we can say that problems don't exist. Here is why:

- **What you don't focus on doesn't exist:** A problem only exists when you give it your attention. From your mind's perspective, what you don't give any thought to doesn't exist. Let's take a hypothetical example. Imagine you lost your legs. If you accept that fact immediately and refuse to give it any thought, there will be no problem and thus, no mental suffering. You would simply be living in reality, (of course, that's usually not what happens).
- **A problem exists only in time:** A problem can only exist in the past or in the future. And where do the past and future exist? In your mind. To acknowledge a problem, you must use your thoughts, and thoughts exist in time, not in the present moment.
- **A problem needs to be labeled as a problem to actually exist:** A problem exists only when you interpret a situation as being a problem. Otherwise, there is no problem.

This concept may be hard to grasp at first, but it's a fundamental theory. In the next section, we'll look at the different components affecting your emotions.

* * *

Action step

Explore the nature of emotions using the workbook (*Section I. What Emotions are - 4. The nature of emotions*).

PART II

WHAT IMPACTS YOUR EMOTIONS

Your mind operates on the famous computing principle of GIGO - garbage in, garbage out. If you do ill, speak ill and think ill, the residue is going to leave you sick. If you do well, speak well and think well, the outcome is going to be well.

— OM SWAMI, A MILLION THOUGHTS.

Emotions are complex, and a variety of factors influence how you feel. In this section, we'll cover some of the elements affecting what drives your emotions. The good news is, you have some control over them.

If we exclude spontaneous emotional reactions resulting from your survival mechanism, most of your emotions are self-created. They result from the way you interpret thoughts or events. However, these aren't the only elements that affect your emotional state. Your body, your voice, the food you eat, or how much you sleep, also play a role in determining the quality of your emotions and therefore the quality of your life.

Let's see how each of these elements impact your emotions.

4

THE IMPACT OF SLEEP ON YOUR MOOD

The quality of your sleep and how much of it you get affects your emotional state. You've probably experienced the side effects of sleep deprivation yourself. Perhaps, you felt grumpy, unable to concentrate, listless, or had difficulty dealing with negative emotions.

Sleep deprivation can impact mood in many different ways.

According to a survey performed on people suffering from anxiety or depression most of the respondents reported receiving less than six hours sleep per night.

Sleep deprivation also increases mortality risk. A 2016 study conducted by researchers at non-profit organization, RAND Europe, estimated that people sleeping less than six hours a night had a thirteen percent increased mortality risk than people sleeping between seven and nine hours. The same studies revealed that lack of sleep cost an estimated $411 billion per year to the United States economy.

Interestingly, sleep deprivation also seems to reduce an individual's ability to enjoy positive experiences. One study shows that, while people who had enough sleep did experience a positive effect from such experiences, no such effect was generated in people who were sleep deprived.

How to improve the quality of your sleep

There are many ways to improve the quality of your sleep. Let's go over some of them:

- **Make sure your bedroom is pitch black.** Many studies have shown that the darker the bedroom is, the better we tend to sleep. If your room isn't pitch-black, what can you do to make it darker? Maybe you can buy a sleep mask, or curtains that do a better job at blocking daylight.
- **Avoid using electronic devices.** This applies to smartphones, tablets, televisions, and the like. According to SleepFoundation.org, "*Studies have shown that even our small electronic devices emit sufficient light to miscue the brain and promote wakefulness. As adults, we are subject to these influences, and our children are particularly susceptible*". A 2014 study published in PNAS showed that melatonin, a chemical which helps regulate sleep patterns, was reduced by fifty percent in participants who read with electronic devices rather than books. These participants took about ten minutes longer to fall asleep and lost ten minutes of deep sleep (also known as REM). Participants also reported feeling less alert in the morning. If your device has a light setting for nighttime use, it may still have a negative impact on your sleep, but just test the night setting and see if it makes a difference to your sleep patterns. If you absolutely *have* to use electronic devices

at night, considering wearing glasses that block the blue light they emit. It's best to put the glasses on a few hours before you go to bed.

- **Relax your mind.** If you're like me, you may have all kinds of thoughts running through your head when it's time to fall asleep. I tend to get very excited about new ideas I have, or things I want to do. As a result, I often feel as though there are so many things I could've completed during the day, and these feelings make it difficult for me to sleep. Aside from turning off electronic devices before bed, I've found that listening to soothing music really helps. Reading a physical book can also help me relax (as long as I don't get too excited by the book, which has been known to happen.)
- **Avoid drinking too much water within two hours of going to bed.** This one is obvious, but still worth mentioning. If you have to go to the bathroom in the middle of the night, it's going to interrupt your sleep pattern. This, of course, will probably make you more tired the next day.
- **Have an evening ritual.** This alone will help you fall asleep more easily. It's best to try going to bed at the same time every night, including the weekends. If you like to go out during the weekend and stay up late, this will present a challenge, but I encourage you to give it a try and see how it goes. An evening ritual will also help you stay on track with your morning ritual. It will be easier to wake up every day at the same time without feeling tired if you have a morning and a nighttime ritual. If you do go out and stay up late during the weekend, one thing you can do is still wake up as early as during the weekdays and have a couple of naps throughout the day as necessary.

If you have difficulty sleeping well, try to implement some of the things mentioned above. The best advice I can give you is to keep trying different strategies until you figure out what works best for you.

5
———

USING YOUR BODY TO INFLUENCE YOUR EMOTIONS

<blockquote>
Our bodies change our minds, our minds change our behavior, and our behavior changes our outcomes.

— AMY CUDDY, SOCIAL PSYCHOLOGIST.
</blockquote>

Body language and body posture

By changing your body language and your body posture you can alter the way you feel. When you are confident or happy you expand your body, and make yourself bigger. Have you noticed how men straighten their backs, expand their chests, and tighten their stomachs when they see an attractive woman? That's an unconscious behavior designed to show confidence and power (the same way gorillas pound their chests).

In one of her experiments, Amy Cuddy, a social psychologist at Harvard Business School, showed that participants who adopted a high-power pose for just two minutes, displayed characteristics similar to those of confident and powerful people. More specifically, she noticed the following hormonal changes.

After adopting a high-power pose for two minutes:

- Testosterone increased by 25%
- Cortisol decreased by 10%, and
- Risk tolerance increased, with 86% of participants choosing to partake in a game of chance.

After adopting a low-power pose for two minutes:

- Testosterone decreased by 10%
- Cortisol increased by 15%, and
- Risk tolerance decreased, with only 60% of participants choosing to partake in a game of chance.

As you can see, you can actually change the way you feel merely by changing your body posture or facial expression. It is what some people call "fake it until you make it." For instance, you can put a smile on your face to make you feel happier. Conversely, you can negatively affect your mood and even create a depression by changing your body posture.

David K. Reynolds, in his book *Constructive Living*, explained how he changed his identity for his alter ego, David Kent, and created a depressed, suicidal patient. The goal was to be accepted as an anonymous patient into various psychiatric facilities to assess them from the inside. Note that he wasn't simulating depression, he was *actually* depressed. Psychological tests proved it. Here is how he created depression:

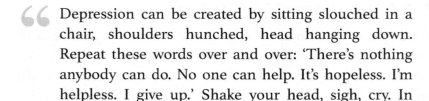 Depression can be created by sitting slouched in a chair, shoulders hunched, head hanging down. Repeat these words over and over: 'There's nothing anybody can do. No one can help. It's hopeless. I'm helpless. I give up.' Shake your head, sigh, cry. In

general, act depressed and the genuine feeling will follow in time.

— DAVID K. REYNOLDS, CONSTRUCTIVE LIVING.

The benefits of exercising

According to Michael Otto, professor of psychology at Boston University, "*Failing to exercise when you feel bad is like explicitly not taking an aspirin when your head hurts.*"

When the time came for 'David Kent' to bring David K. Reynolds back to life, what do you think he needed to do? He needed to change his body position. Easy to say but hard to do when you're clinically depressed. Of course, he knew that better than anybody else. Still, he had to force himself to become physically active, despite not wanting to do so. As he started increasing his physical activity and getting busy, he felt better and better until he fully recovered.

David Kent's story shows that regular exercising improves, not only your physical well-being, but also your mood. Studies have shown that exercising can treat mild to moderate depression as effectively as antidepressants. In one study, James Blumenthal, a clinical psychologist at Duke University, assigned sedentary adults with major depressive disorders to one of four groups: supervised exercise, home-based exercise, antidepressant therapy, or a placebo pill. After four months Blumenthal found that patients in the exercise and antidepressant group had the highest rates of remission. In his conclusions, he stated that exercise has more or less the same effect as antidepressants.

When he followed up with the same patients a year later, Blumenthal discovered that people who were still exercising regularly had lower depression scores than people who only exercised sporadically. Exercise seems to not only help treat depression, but also to prevent relapse. So, when it comes to mastering your emotions, make sure exercising is part of your toolbox.

Fortunately, you don't have to run ten miles a day to reap the benefits of exercise. Simply walking for thirty minutes, five days a week can work wonders. According to research published in PLoS Medicine, two and a half hours moderate exercise a week could add three and a quarter years to your lifespan. Another study of five thousand people in Denmark showed that individuals who exercised regularly lived five to seven years longer than sedentary counterparts.

As for the benefits of exercising on your mood, they are both immediate and long-term. Professor of psychology, Michael Otto, says you usually derive a mood enhancement effect within five minutes of partaking in moderate exercise. And, as we've just seen, exercising regularly improves your long-term mental health and can be as effective as antidepressants.

What about you? What activity are you going to take on to improve your mental and physical health?

6

USING YOUR THOUGHTS TO INFLUENCE YOUR EMOTIONS

 You become what you think about all day long.

— RALPH WALDO EMERSON, ESSAYIST AND POET.

Your thoughts define who you are and create your reality. That's why you should channel your thoughts towards what you *want*, not what you *don't want*. As the success expert Brian Tracy says, *"The key to success is to focus our conscious mind on things we desire, not things we fear."*

The benefits of meditation

In Buddhism, the mind is often referred to as the "monkey mind," because, Buddhists believe human thoughts are similar to a monkey relentlessly swinging through trees. They are all over the place and never seem to stop. Meditation helps tame the monkey and cure it of restlessness. As you meditate, you become aware of the incessant flow of thoughts popping into your mind. With practice, you learn to distance yourself from thoughts, reducing their power and their impact. As a result, you'll experience less negative emotions and feel more at peace.

The benefits of visualization

Did you know your subconscious can't clearly distinguish real experiences from 'fake' ones? This means you can trick your mind by simulating desired experiences through visualization. The more details you visualize, the more your brain will interpret the experience as real.

By using visualization to elicit positive feelings such as gratitude, excitement, or joy, you can condition your mind to experience more positive emotions, as we'll see in more depth in the section "Conditioning your mind."

7

USING YOUR WORDS TO INFLUENCE YOUR EMOTIONS

Your words have more impact on your thoughts and behaviors than you might realize. Because your thoughts, words, and behaviors are all interconnected, they influence each other. For instance, when you lack confidence, you use certain words such as "I'll try," "I hope," or "I wish." Conversely, using specific words can make you feel less confident. This also means you can boost your confidence by using certain words such as, "I will." For instance, saying "I will change career," or "I will complete this project by the end of this month," will make you feel more confident than saying, "I hope I can change career," or "I'll try to complete this project by the end of this month."

To enhance your confidence, replace words that show self-doubt with words that display confidence as shown below.

Words to be avoided:

- Would/could/should/might
- Try/hope/wish
- Maybe/perhaps

- If everything is okay
- If everything goes well

Words to be used instead:

- I will
- Absolutely
- Definitely
- Of course
- Sure
- Certainly
- Obviously
- Without any doubt
- No problem

The power of positive affirmations

Positive affirmations are sentences you repeat to yourself on a regular basis until your subconscious mind accepts them as true. Over time they help you condition your mind to experience positive emotions such as confidence or gratitude. For more information on how to condition your mind refer to the section, 'Conditioning your mind.'

How to use positive affirmation

- Use the present tense and not the future tense, ("I am" not "I will").
- Avoid negative forms like "I am not shy." Instead, use "I am confident."
- Repeat the sentence again and again for five minutes.
- Do it every single day without exception for a month, and preferably longer.
- Use visualization at the same time and involve your emotions.

Some examples of powerful affirmations:

- I love being confident.
- I am independent of the good or bad opinions of others.
- I am beneath no one and no one is beneath me.
- I love you .... (add your name and say it while looking into your eyes in the mirror, e.g. "I love you, Thibaut".) Awkward, isn't it?
- Thank you.

Exercise

- Use positive affirmation for five minutes daily.
- Notice words that show a lack of commitment, confidence or assertiveness. Go over your emails before you send them and remove phrases such as, "I'll try," "I should," "I hope," etc. Replace them with, "I will" or something equally assertive. For the next three weeks, challenge yourself to avoid using words showing a lack of confidence.

Additional tip:

The world-famous life coach, Tony Robbins, has been using what he calls "incantation," for decades before meeting a client or holding a seminar. He uses both his body and certain phrases to put himself in the right state and to reach a level of absolute certainty. As you perform your own affirmations, try engaging your body as well. Remember, your words *and* your body affect your emotions.

8

HOW YOUR BREATHING AFFECTS YOUR EMOTIONS

You can stay without food or sleep for days, but you cannot survive past a few minutes without oxygen. While breathing should happen naturally, the truth is that many people don't know how to breathe properly. As a result, they don't generate as much energy as they could. These individuals tire more easily than others, which affects their mood and make them more prone to experience negative emotions.

Proper breathing benefits you in different ways. Slowing your breathing helps reduce anxiety. In *Breathwalk: Breathing Your Way to a Revitalized Body, Mind and Spirit,* Gurucharan Singh Khalsa and Yogi Bahjan mentioned the following benefits from slow breathing:

- *Eight breathing cycles per minute*: Relief from stress and increased awareness.
- *Four breathing cycles per minute*: Intense feelings of awareness, increased visual clarity, heightened bodily sensitivity.
- *One breathing cycle per minute*: Optimized cooperation

between brain hemispheres, dramatic calming of anxiety, fear, and worry.

Rapid breathing such as the Breath of Fire, allows you to release stress, be more alert and have more energy alongside other benefits. (You can watch a tutorial video by searching 'Breath of Fire' on YouTube).

For more on how to use breathing to change your mood you can refer to *Breathwalk: Breathing Your Way to a Revitalized Body, Mind and Spirit* or search out other books on breathing.

9

HOW YOUR ENVIRONMENT AFFECTS YOUR EMOTIONS

Your environment also influences the way you feel. By environment, I mean everything around you can affect you in some way. It could be people you hang out with, TV shows you watch, or the place you live. For instance, negative relatives may drag you down, while a messy desk may be demotivating.

I've noticed that when I feel demotivated, decluttering my desk, cleaning my room, or reorganizing files on my computer often gives me a boost of motivation.

For more on how you can use your environment to change your emotions see the section, 'Changing your Environment.'

10

HOW MUSIC AFFECTS YOUR EMOTIONS

We all know music affects our mood. Who hasn't listened to Rocky's song while working out? For instance, music can:

- Help you relax when you're tired
- Motivate you when you're in a slump
- Help you persevere when you're at the gym
- Help you access feelings of gratitude, and
- Put you in a positive mood state.

Some studies have shown that listening to positive music can help people boost their mood. In a study conducted in 2012, participants reported higher positive mood after listening to a positive song for just twelve minutes, five times, over a two-week period. Interestingly, it only worked with participants who were told to make an effort to boost their mood. Other participants didn't report such mood improvement.

Another study conducted in 2014 showed that music can help reduce negative mood and boost self-esteem as indicated below:

> Specifically, the most significant results of the music interventions on the psychological side can be identified in the aspects more closely related to mood, especially in the reduction of the depressive and anxiety's component, and in the improvement of the emotional expression, communication and interpersonal skills, self-esteem and quality of life.

Valerie N. Stratton, Ph.D. and Annette H. Zalanowski, of Penn State University, also studied the effect of music on mood. They asked their students to keep music diaries for two weeks. Stratton concluded that:

> Not only did our sample of students report more positive emotions after listening to music, but their already positive emotions were intensified by listening to music.

Interestingly, the music genre and the context in which students listened to the music didn't affect the result. Students' mood improved whether they listened to rock or classical music, or whether they were at home, driving, or socializing.

Using music to condition your mind

You can go one step further and use the power of music to condition your mind by creating playlists tailored to your emotional needs. Building playlists is time-consuming, but well worth the effort. The world-class endurance athlete and coach, Christopher Bergland, uses music to help him stay motivated and perform at his best. This is what he wrote in an article published in *Psychology Today*:

As an athlete, I developed an ideal mindset for peak performance and used an arsenal of time-tested songs to fortify this alter ego and invincible state of mind. During my training and races it became obvious that even in really horrible weather conditions, or when I was physically suffering, that I could use music (and my imagination) to create a parallel universe that had little to do with reality. I used music to stay optimistic and see the glass as perpetually half-full while doing ultra-endurance races. You can use music as a tool when you work out or in your daily life the same way.

Christopher also enjoys listening to specific songs before a big interview or when he does public speaking. Personally, I like to listen to songs that make me feel grateful. What about you? How can you use music to improve your mood?

Exercise - Experiment with different types of music.

Experiment with different types of music and see how you can use them to boost your mood. For instance, you could use music to help you meditate, work out, or do your homework. As you do so, keep the following points in mind:

- **Everybody is different**: don't listen to a song because it's popular. Listen to it because it makes you feel the way you want to feel. We all have different musical tastes. The only thing that matters is how *you* feel when you listen to music.
- **Keep experimenting**: Listen to different types of music and see how they make you feel. Are you inspired? Motivated? Happy? Relaxed? Start creating playlists for specific moods you want to experience.

* * *

Action step

Use the workbook to design new strategies to better take control of your emotions (*Section II. What impact your emotions*).

PART III

HOW TO CHANGE YOUR EMOTIONS

The mind always seeks to deny the Now and to escape from it. In other words, the more you are identified with your mind, the more you suffer. Or you may put it like this: the more you are able to honor and accept the Now, the more you are free of pain, of suffering—and free of the egoic mind.

— ECKHART TOLLE, THE POWER OF NOW.

In this section, we'll explore how you can deal with negative emotions and condition your mind to experience more positive ones.

First, we'll discuss how emotions are formed. Then, we'll discuss the benefit of positive thinking and how to use it to condition your mind. After that, we'll see why positive thinking isn't enough and what else you can do to deal with negative emotions. More specifically, you'll learn:

- How to let go of your emotions

- How to change your story and create a more empowering one
- How to condition your mind
- How to use your behaviors to change your emotions, and
- How to modify your environment to reduce negative emotions.

Finally, I'll share with you a list of short-term and long-term strategies you can use to better deal with negative emotions.

Let's get started.

11

HOW EMOTIONS ARE FORMED

> When a thought emerges on the canvas of your mind, if you don't drop it, its pursuit will either take the form of a desire or an emotion, positive or negative.

— OM SWAMI, A MILLION THOUGHTS.

Few people know how emotions are formed. While we experience them all day long, we seldom—if ever—take time to understand why we are feeling certain emotions and how they came into existence.

First, let's differentiate two types of negative emotions. The first type are the negative emotions you experience spontaneously. These are the emotions that keep you alive such as the fear our ancestors felt when they encountered a saber-tooth tiger.

The second type of negative emotions are the ones you create in your mind by identifying with your thoughts. These emotions aren't necessarily triggered by external events—although they may be. These emotions tend to last longer than the first type. Here is how they work:

A random thought arises. You identify with that thought. This identification creates an emotional reaction. As you keep identifying with that thought, the related emotion grows stronger until it becomes a core emotion. Let's look at some examples:

- You have money problems, and each time your mind comes up with money-related thoughts you identify with them. As a result, your worry about money intensifies.
- You had an argument with your friend and fell out with him. You can't stop replaying the scene in your mind. As a result, months have passed and you still haven't called to make up with your friend.
- You made a mistake at work and are ashamed of yourself. You keep revisiting the same thought over and over. As a result, your feelings of inadequacy grow stronger.

Your tendency to identify with negative thoughts repeatedly is what allows them to grow stronger. The more you focus on your financial challenges, the easier it will be for related thoughts to arise in the future. The more you replay the argument with your friend in your head, the stronger the feelings of resentment will grow. Similarly, as you keep thinking of the mistake you made at work, you invite feelings of shame and intensify the situation. The point is, when you give thoughts room to exist, they spread and become major points of focus.

This simple process of identification allows seemingly inoffensive thoughts to take control of your mind. This identification with your thoughts, and more importantly, how you choose to interpret them, creates suffering in your life.

Now, let's see in more detail how your emotions are formed. This will help you better deal with negative emotions while allowing positive emotions to grow. Here is a formula to explain how emotions form:

Interpretation + identification + repetition = strong emotion

- **Interpretation:** is when you interpret an event or a thought based on your personal story.
- **Identification:** is when you identify with a specific thought as it arises.
- **Repetition:** is having the same thoughts over and over.
- **Strong emotion:** is when you experience an emotion so many times it has become part of your identity. You then experience that emotion whenever a related thought or event triggers it.

Altogether, interpretation, identification and repetition give room for emotions to grow. Conversely, whenever you remove one of these elements from the equation, these emotions start losing their power over you.

To sum up, for an emotion to grow in intensity and duration, you must first interpret an event or a thought, then, you must identify with that thought as it arises, finally, you must repeat the same thoughts again and again—and identify with it.

Now, let's discuss in more depth each component of the formula.

1. Interpretation

Interpretation + identification + repetition = strong emotion

Negative emotions always result from your interpretation of events. That's why two different people might react to the same event in different ways. One might be devastated, while the other might be unaffected.

For instance, for a farmer rain could be a blessing, but for someone going on a picnic it would be seen as a curse. That's because of the meaning they give to the event. **In short, for negative emotions to arise, you must add your interpretation to a specific event.** The event in itself cannot trigger negative emotions without your consent.

So, why do you keep experiencing negative emotions? I believe it's because reality fails to meet your expectations.

- You want reality to be one way, but it turns out to be another.
- You go on a picnic and want the weather to be good, but it rains.
- You want a promotion at work, but you don't get it.
- You want to make money with your side business, but it's not working.

Your interpretation of reality creates suffering in your life. Reality in itself can never be upsetting. This is worth repeating. We'll discuss in depth how you can change your interpretation in the next section entitled, 'Changing your story.'

2. Identification

Interpretation + **identification** + repetition = strong emotion

Now, let's focus on the second part of the formula: identification.

For an emotion to survive long term, there must be a process of identification. Emotions cannot persist unless you give them your attention. The more you focus on your emotions—and identify with them—the more powerful they become.

People often feel the urge to identify with their emotions and find themselves unable to disengage from them. They fail to realize one of the most important truths in this world: **you are not your emotions.** Your emotions *will* come and they *will* go.

So, when you catch yourself saying, "I'm sad," remember you are incorrect. Nobody has ever been sad, because your emotions are not who you are. They can *appear* to be you, but they will soon disappear, like clouds in the sky. Think of yourself as the sun, and the sun is always there whether or not you perceive it—whether or not its hidden by the cloud.

You are not your emotions. You are *not* sad, you merely *experience feelings* that you may call 'sadness' at a given point in time. This is an important point. I hope you can see the difference.

Another way to see your emotions is as the clothes you wear. What emotional clothes are you wearing right now? Are they clothes of excitement? Depression? Sadness? Bear in mind, tomorrow, or a week from now, you will likely be wearing different clothes.

How long you wear your clothes (your emotions) depends on how much you love them (i.e. how much you're attached to your emotions). An emotion in itself is powerless. What gives it power is your conscious or unconscious identification with it. That's why an emotion given no attention will eventually fade away. Try the following exercise:

Whenever you're angry, get busy with any activity requiring your full attention. You'll see your anger quickly dissipate. Conversely, keep dwelling on the feelings of anger, and you'll see it grow until it becomes one of your major emotional states.

3. Repetition

Interpretation + identification + **repetition** = strong emotion

We've seen that the way you interpret an event or a thought

59

determines how you feel. We also know that, as you identify with your thoughts or feelings, they become emotions. Now, if you keep repeating that process, you'll condition your mind to experience these specific emotions (positive or negative).

For instance, if you focus your attention on what (you believe) your friend did to you, feelings of resentment will grow. As a result, you could hold a grudge for months. People often do this. They waste time holding onto negative emotions that serve no purpose just because they can't let go of them.

Conversely, if you disengage from your thoughts of resentment and simply observe them, over time they will lose power and the associated resentment will fade away. In fact, if you had let go of the thought of resentment immediately after it arose, your feelings of resentment would have dissipated almost instantly. We'll see how you can let go of your emotion in the section, 'Letting go of your emotions.'

* * *

Action step

Resist negative emotions from the past using the workbook, (*Section III. How to change your emotions - 1. How emotions are formed*).

Recall the last time you felt anger, sadness, frustration, fear, or depression. Now, write down what happens for each of the following:

- Interpretation: What events happened and what thoughts arose?
- Identification: How did you respond to these thoughts?
- Repetition: Did you identify with these thoughts repeatedly?

12

CHANGING YOUR INTERPRETATION

> The sight of a slaughterhouse may trigger a negative emotion in you, whereas it may be positive for the business owner and natural for the machine operator. It all depends on how you are conditioned.
>
> — OM SWAMI, A MILLION THOUGHTS.

In itself, an event or a thought has no power to alter your emotional state. What generates emotions is the way you choose to interpret the event or thought. This is why two people can react differently to the same situation. One will see a problem and blame external circumstances, while the other will see an opportunity to be embraced. One will get stuck, the other will grow.

The way you interpret events is closely linked to general assumptions you hold about life. As such, it is essential we first delve into the underlying assumptions that lead to these interpretations.

Exploring your assumptions

To enter a given emotional state, you made certain assumptions regarding how things should be. These assumptions constitute your subjective reality. Because you're convinced they are true, you don't question them.

Below are some examples of assumptions you may have:

- Problems should be avoided
- This is a problem
- I should be healthy
- I'll live at least until I'm seventy
- I must get married
- Complaining is normal
- There is nothing wrong with dwelling on the past
- I need to worry about the future, and/or
- I can't be happy unless or until *insert your answer(s) here*.

Now, let's look at each one of these assumptions:

Problems should be avoided: Many people want to get rid of their problems. But what if you can't, and what if you don't need to? For sure, some people have 'better' problems than others, but everybody has problems. What if the assumption that you shouldn't have any problems is wrong? What if you need to learn how to dance in the rain and make the most of your problems? What if problems are just challenges to be overcome—and part of life.

This is a problem: What if this thing you label as a problem is actually not a problem? What if it doesn't matter as much as you think? What if it's an opportunity in disguise? And how could you make it so?

I should be healthy: We tend to take our health for granted, but we cannot guarantee we won't get sick tomorrow. What if your health is a blessing and not necessarily the default position? Wouldn't that make you think of your health in a different way?

I'll live at least until I'm seventy: You probably assume you'll live a long life, but what if that's not the case? Isn't living a long life a blessing rather than something you should take for granted? Unfortunately, some people die young, but that's the nature of reality. People say, "He died too young," but is that correct? Isn't it more accurate to say that he just died? Neither too young nor too old.

I must get married. Maybe, maybe not. That's just your interpretation. 'Shoulds' are generally things society or your parents expect you to do, but it doesn't mean it has to be that way. These are often cultural norms or conditioned behaviors.

Complaining is normal: Most complaining is a play of the ego and is not constructive. It doesn't help you and doesn't change anything. The only thing it does is strengthen your ego and offend people. Try to spend an entire week without complaining and see what happens.

There is nothing wrong with dwelling on the past: You probably spend (too much) time dwelling on the past. Everybody does. But do you realize the past exists only in your mind? And do you realize you can't change it no matter what you do? Learning from your past is useful, dwelling on it isn't.

I need to worry about the future: Worrying about the future is unavoidable to a certain extent but it doesn't help. Instead, you should do the best you can in the present to avoid future problems.

I can't be happy unless *insert your answer(s)*: You don't need to have the perfect life to be happy. Happiness is a choice you need to make every day. You must practice it since, as we've seen before, external factors won't significantly affect your happiness.

These are just some examples of assumptions you may hold. My intention here is to show you that your interpretations—and the emotions generated from them—are largely the result of the assumptions you hold about the world. Thus, to experience more positive emotions, it is important you spend time revising your assumptions.

Analyzing your interpretations

As we've already seen, you interpret events based on your assumptions. Now, below are some questions to help you understand what I mean by interpretations.

- Do you think everything happens for a reason and embrace it, or
- Do you play the victim?

- Do you believe temporary setbacks are just milestones that will lead you to succeed, or
- Do you give up when you encounter your first major setback?

- Do you try to change things that cannot be changed, or
- Do you accept them?

- Do you believe you're here for a reason, or
- Do you wander through life without any clear purpose?

- Do you believe problems are bad and should be avoided, or
- Do you believe they are a necessary part of life?

Remember, what differentiates people who live a happy life from people who are miserable is often how they choose to interpret their lives.

* * *

Action step

Write down interpretations of your emotions using the workbook, (*Section III. How to change your emotions - 2. Changing your story*).

Write down:

- One or two emotional issues you currently have. (Ask yourself, "If I could get rid of some emotions, losing which ones would have the most positive impact on my life?")
- Your interpretation of these issues. (Ask yourself, "What would I need to believe for my story to be true?")
- New empowering interpretations that will help you deal with these issues. (Ask yourself, "What do I need to believe to avoid experiencing these negative emotions?")

13

LETTING GO OF YOUR EMOTIONS

66 Emotions are just emotions. They are not you, they are not facts, and you can let them go.

— Hale Dworkin, The Sedona Method.

As we've seen, interpretation, identification and repetition can lead to the creation of strong emotions. In this section, we'll see what you can do to start letting go of emotions that aren't helping you achieve the life you want.

E-motions are energy in motion, but what happens when you prevent the energy from moving? It accumulates. When you repress your emotions, you interrupt the natural flow of energy.

Sadly, nobody taught you how to deal with your emotions or even that both, positive *and* negative emotions, are a natural phenomenon. Instead, they told you that your negative emotions should be repressed because they are bad.

As a result, you may have been repressing your emotions for years. By doing so, you let them sink deeper into your subconscious, allowing them to become part of your identity. They have often become patterns you may be unaware of. For instance, perhaps, you feel you aren't good enough. Or maybe you experience guilt on a regular basis. These are the results of core beliefs you developed over time by repressing your emotions.

Most of us have too much emotional baggage and need to learn to let go of it. We need to declutter our subconscious and get rid of the negative emotions preventing us from enjoying life to the fullest.

The fact is, your subconscious is already programmed to help you deal with life. Your subconscious ensures you don't accidentally forget to breathe, keeps your heart beating and regulates your body temperature among millions of other things. It doesn't need additional beliefs to function well. Neither does it need to 'store' emotions.

If you're like most people, you spend the majority of your time living in your head. As a result, you're largely out of touch with your emotions. To start letting go of your emotions, you must first become aware of them by becoming more in touch with your body and the way you feel.

Below are a few simple steps you can take to start letting go of your emotions.

1. Observe your emotions with detachment

Whenever you experience a negative emotion, simply observe it with as much detachment as you can. That means getting in touch with your body. Realize that each thought or image crossing your mind isn't the emotion itself, it's only your interpretation of it. Practice feeling how it feels. Try to locate the emotion. Think of the way you would describe the emotion to someone else. Remember, don't:

- Engage in a story revolving around that emotion, and
- Believe in whatever images or thoughts that arise when you experience that emotion.

2. Label your emotion

Remember, emotions are merely temporary experiences, or if you prefer, clothes you wear for a while. They aren't 'you.'

When you experience an emotion you say things like, "I am angry," "I am sad," or "I am depressed." Notice how you instantly identify with your emotions. However, this is factually incorrect. The emotions you experience have nothing to do with who you really are. If you were your depression, you'll be depressed all day long every single second of your existence. Fortunately, that's not the case.

Let's assume you feel sad. Rather than saying, "I'm sad," a more accurate way to describe that emotion would be: "I feel sad," or "I experience a feeling of sadness."

Can you see how different it is from saying, "I'm sad?" It gives you more space to distance yourself from your emotions. The more you become aware of your emotions, the more you can label them and detach yourself from them, and the easier it will be to let go of these emotions.

3. Let go of your emotions

Too often, you over-identify with your emotions and cling to them for the following reasons:

- They're part of the story you're telling yourself. Sometimes, you can't stop clinging to a story even a disempowering one. Yes, you can become addicted to destructive stories despite knowing they aren't helping you.

- You believe the emotions are *you* and feel a strong need to identify with them. You may fall into the trap of believing you are your emotions. As a result, you identify heavily with them, which creates suffering.

Real life example:

I regularly felt that I wasn't good enough. As a result, I believed I should work harder. This belief led me to create lists of daily goals that were impossible to complete even when working from morning to night. I often fell short on my goals, which reinforced the belief that I wasn't good enough.

By realizing this was just a story, I started letting go of this belief. After doing so, I noticed I was actually getting almost as much work done but without the need to struggle and feel stressed out. I'm still working on that issue, but I gain tremendous value from this process.

The challenging part was to let go of the attachment to my story by letting go of the following:

- The belief that I'm not good enough and must work harder
- The pride I feel from working harder than most people
- The victim mentality that comes from working hard while not getting the results I want
- The idea I'm somewhat 'special'
- The idea the world needs to be changed, and
- The need to control the outcome of my actions.

As you can see, letting go of core emotions is not easy. They've become part of our identity, and we often derive a twisted pleasure from them. We may even wonder who we will be without them.

4. A five-step process to let go of emotions

In his book, *The Sedona Method*, Hale Dwoskin explains there are three different ways to release your emotions as they arise. You can:

1. Let them go. When you experience negative emotions, you can consciously choose to release them rather than repressing them or clinging to them
2. Allow them to be here. You can allow them by acknowledging their existence without clinging to them, or you can
3. Welcome them. You can accept them and have a closer look at them to discover what the core of these emotions are.

According to Hale Dwoskin, the first step in each case is to become aware of your emotions as they arise. He then introduces a five-step process to let go of your emotions:

Step 1: Focus on a certain emotion you would like to work on so you can feel better. This doesn't need to be a 'big' emotion. It could be something as simple as not feeling like working on a specific task, or being mildly annoyed about something.

Step 2: ask yourself one of the following questions:

1. Could I let this feeling go?
2. Could I allow this feeling to be here?
3. Could I welcome this feeling?

Depending on which way you want to go (release, allow, or welcome), answer the corresponding question.

Step 3: Then ask yourself, "Would I?"

1. Would I let this feeling go?
2. Would I allow this feeling to be here?
3. Would I welcome this feeling?

Answer yes or no to each question while being honest with yourself. Do you feel like you can let go/allow/welcome the emotion? Even a 'no' will help you let go of it.

Step 4: Ask yourself, "When"?

Your answer will be, "Now." You let go of that emotion immediately.

Step 5: Repeat this process as many times as necessary for that particular feeling to disappear.

You may be tempted to brush off this technique as overly simplistic and ineffective. Don't do that! Try it for yourself. Remember that you are *not* your emotions. That's precisely by practicing letting go of them that you'll realize that universal truth. As you make a conscious choice to let go of your emotions, welcome them fully or allow them to be, you'll gain a whole new understanding of how emotions work and how to release them.

* * *

Action step

Use the exercises in the corresponding section of the workbook to start letting go of your emotions, (*Section III. How emotions are formed - 3. Letting go of your emotions*).

Make a list of all the emotions you would like to let go of. Perhaps you feel as though you aren't good enough. Perhaps you struggle with procrastination and experience guilt and shame. Maybe you blame yourself for something you did in the past, or you worry about your future. Just write down whatever comes to your mind. Now, use the method mentioned above.

Select one emotion then ask yourself:

- "Could I let this feeling go?"
- "Would I?" (Yes/no)
- "When?" (Now)

Don't worry if you're not successful at first. You'll have plenty of opportunities to practice in the future.

14

CONDITIONING YOUR MIND TO EXPERIENCE MORE POSITIVE EMOTIONS

> Try to see that a thought about a person or event is merely a thought about that person or event. It is the thought about them that makes you feel the way you do. To change the way you feel, change the way you think.

— Vernon Howard, The Power of Your Supermind.

We've discussed how emotions are formed and we've introduced a process you can use to release your negative emotions. Now, let's see how you can condition your mind to start experiencing and intensifying positive emotions in your life.

You are what you think about most of the time

For thousands of years mystics have told us we are the results of our thoughts. Buddha allegedly said, *"What you think, you become."*

The essayist and poet, Ralph Waldo Emerson, said, *"We become what we think about all day long,"* while Mahatma Gandhi said, *"A man is but the product of his thoughts."*

In his classic book, *As a Man Thinketh,* James Allen wrote,

 Let a man radically alter his thoughts, and he will be astonished at the rapid transformation it will effect in the material conditions of his life. Men imagine that thought can be kept secret, but it cannot; it rapidly crystallizes into habit, and habit solidifies into circumstance.

— JAMES ALLEN

To take control of your emotions, it is essential you understand the role your thoughts play in generating emotions in general. Your thoughts activate certain emotions, and these emotions, in turn, generate more thoughts. Thoughts and emotions then feed each other.

For instance, if believed, the thought, "I'm not good enough," will generate negative emotions such as shame or guilt. Conversely, when you feel ashamed for 'not being good enough,' you'll attract more thoughts in line with that belief. You will focus on the things (you believe) you aren't good at, or remember and dwell on past failures. This in turn will strengthen your erroneous belief.

Thoughts generate emotions and emotions dictate your actions. If you feel you don't deserve a promotion, you won't ask for it. If you believe a man or woman is 'out of your league,' you won't ask him or her out.

In a nutshell, this is the way thoughts work. They generate emotions that dictate your actions and shape your reality. While this may not be obvious to you in the short-term, in the long-term, you'll realize your thoughts have a tremendous impact on your life.

Thoughts and emotions determine your future

Humans possess a power no other living beings have: their imagination. We can use our thoughts to manifest things and turn the invisible into the visible.

However, a thought in itself isn't enough to manifest things or circumstances. It must be fueled with an energy in the form of emotion, such as enthusiasm, excitement, passion, or happiness. For this reason, someone enthusiastic about his or her dream will achieve more than a pessimistic and unmotivated person.

Successful people constantly focus on what they want—with positive expectation—while unsuccessful people focus on what they don't want or what they lack. The latter are afraid of having a lack of money, talent, time, or any other resources they may need to achieve their goals. As a result, pessimists accomplish far less than they're capable of achieving.

Thus, one of the most important skills you can master is your ability to control your thoughts and emotions. This entails understanding what your emotions are, how they work, and what purpose they serve. Later, we'll discuss how you can use your emotions as a tool for personal growth.

Depositing positive thoughts in your mind

Confident people deposit positive thoughts in their mind each day. They celebrate their small wins and treat themselves with compassion and respect. Naturally, they expect good things to happen. On the other hand, people with low self-esteem bombard their mind with disempowering thoughts. They discard their accomplishments as 'no big deal' and fail to recognize their strengths and the positive intent behind their actions. No wonder they feel unworthy. (For more information read section, 'Not being good enough.')

Both use their thoughts to distort reality, but who do you think is better off? The person who deposits positive thoughts in their mind, or the person who dwells on negative thoughts?

Does it mean positive thinking is going to solve all your problems and eliminate your negative emotions once and for all? Of course, not. Thought manipulation is simply one of the tools you can use to master your emotions.

The limit of positive thinking

Repeating to yourself, "I'm happy, I'm happy, I'm happy," all day long won't turn you into a living Buddha. You may benefit from it, but you'll still experience negative emotions. Unless you know how to deal with negative emotions when they appear, you'll fall prey to your own disempowering story. This story could be why you're such a loser or why *insert your favorite disempowering story here*.

Interestingly, people are often addicted to their story—even the negative ones—and are unable to let go of the 'why', because they:

- Are fundamentally flawed
- Will never be happy because *insert your favorite story*
- Aren't worthy of love
- Are never going to make it, and
- Will never get married, and so on.

I can guarantee you are addicted to a story. Now we'll discuss how you can condition your mind to experience more positive emotions. After that, we'll see how you can deal with negative emotions as they arise.

Choosing the emotion(s) you want to experience

To condition your mind, the first step is to decide what emotion(s) you want to experience more of. Do you want to be happier? More motivated? More proactive? The second step is to put in place a specific program to allow you to experience your chosen emotion(s). The final step is to practice feeling that emotion every day.

Feeling the same emotion over and over allows you to better access it. Neuroscience has shown that experiencing the same thought or emotion repeatedly, strengthens the corresponding neural pathways, easing future access to that thought or emotion. Put it simply, the more you experience an emotion, the easier it becomes to generate. That's where daily conditioning comes into play.

To condition your mind to experience positive emotions, you can use the method we introduced earlier:

Interpretation + identification + repetition = strong emotion

Here is how to use the formula in this situation:

- **Interpretation**: Visualizing certain events or generating particular thoughts you see as positive.
- **Identification**: Identifying with these events or thoughts by feeling the way you want to feel. To do this you can use all the techniques we mentioned in the section, 'What impacts your emotions,' such as positive affirmations and visualization.
- **Repetition**: Keep repeating the same thoughts and

identifying with them. By doing so, you allow your mind to access the related emotions more easily.

Below are some examples of practices you can use based on how you want to feel:

1. Gratitude

To feel more grateful, make gratitude a daily routine. Every morning, focus on what you're grateful for. The more you practice, the better you'll be able to focus on the positive side of things. Sadly, most of us know we should be grateful, but we aren't. That's why we must cultivate gratitude. As the late Jim Rohn said, *"Our emotions need to be as educated as our intellect."*

Here are some exercises you can use to cultivate a feeling of gratitude:

A. Write down things you're grateful for: Take a pen and a piece of paper, or even better, a dedicated notebook, and write down at least three things for which you are grateful. This will help you focus on the positive side of things.

B. Thank people who crossed your life: Close your eyes and think of people you've met. As you picture them one after the other, thank them while acknowledging at least one good thing they did for you. If you happen to picture people you don't like, thank them anyway and still look for one good thing they did for you. It could be making you stronger or teaching you a specific lesson. Don't try to control your thoughts, simply let the faces of people you know come to your mind. Release any resentment you feel or have felt.

C. Focus on one object and appreciate its existence:

- Select one item in your room and think of the amount of

work and number of people involve in the process of creating it and delivering it to you. For instance, if you select a chair, think of all the work necessary to create it. Some people had to design it, others had to find raw materials, and others had to assemble it. Truck drivers had to deliver it to the store. The store employees had to display it and promote it. You or someone else had to go and collect it. The car you drive also had to be built by other people, and so on.

- Think of how you benefit from this chair: Remember a time you were so tired you couldn't wait to sit. Didn't it feel great when you could finally sit? Thanks to the chair you can not only sit, but you can also use your computer, write, read, drink coffee, or have a pleasant conversation with your friends.

D. Listening to gratitude song/guided meditation: Listen to gratitude meditation. (Search, 'gratitude meditation' on YouTube)

2. Excitement

Sometimes, you lose excitement. You feel as though you're running in circles trapped in the same old routine. To generate more excitement, spend a little time every morning visualizing all the things you want. Get excited about these things. Below are several ways to do it, (please note, this should be practiced on a regular basis):

A. Write down what you want: Take a pen and piece of paper and write, 'What I Want,' at the top of the page. Then, write down anything you can think of that excites you.

B. Visualize what you want: Ask yourself, "What do I really want?" and visualize all the things you desire. Try to be as specific as possible. Clarity is power. Think of your ideal career, relationship or lifestyle, or any goals you want to accomplish in the coming decade or beyond.

C. Create a goals/dreams journal: Buy a notebook and write down your goals in each area of your life. Review them each morning and keep adding pictures, drawings or anything else to foster your enthusiasm.

D. Vividly envision your ideal day:

- What would you eat for breakfast?
- How would you spend your day?
- With whom would you spend your day?
- What would you do in the evening?
- Where would you live?
- How would you feel?

You can have several versions of your ideal day. Just make sure each version excites you.

3. Confidence/certainty

If you want to have more confidence in your ability to achieve your goals, visualize yourself as having already accomplished them, and feel good about it. Practice developing a sense of certainty. Commit to your vision in your mind. Each time you visualize your goal, give the energy of commitment to it. *Know* it's going to happen.

4. Self-esteem

To boost your self-esteem, keep track of your daily accomplishments. You do many things right, but you tend only to remember things you do wrong. No wonder your self-esteem suffers. Buy a notebook and dedicate it to this purpose. Record your accomplishments every day. Some examples of accomplishments would be:

- I woke on time
- I ate some fruit
- I cleaned my desk
- I completed Project A
- I exercised
- I completed my morning ritual, and/or
- I read.

As you can see, you don't have to write down anything big. In fact, by writing down small accomplishments, you condition your mind to look for more wins, which, over time, enhances your self-esteem.

For more exercises related to self-esteem refer to the section: 'Not feeling good enough.'

5. Decisiveness

As you practice being more decisive, you'll boost your productivity, which will affect your well-being. As we'll see in the section, 'Procrastination,' stalling can create a lot of emotional suffering.

To become more decisive, you can use the **5 Second Rule**, introduced by Mel Robbins in her book of the same name. In it, Mel Robbins argues there is only one rule when it comes to productivity, success, or getting everything you ever wanted: you have to do something whether you feel like it or not. If you can do the things you don't feel like doing, you'll get everything you've ever wanted.

Her **5 Second Rule** states you have five seconds from the moment you have an idea to the moment you take action. If you fail to act within these five seconds, your mind will talk you out of it. The nature of the mind is to prevent us from doing anything scary or tiring. For instance, you have five seconds to:

- Introduce yourself to someone you want to talk to at an event
- Send that important email, or
- Ask a question during a meeting.

Exercise - Strengthen your decisiveness

To practice the **5 Second Rule,** you can start with small things.

- Make a list of things you procrastinate over. Perhaps you put off washing the dishes, or cleaning your home. Maybe, you delay calling someone or sending some emails. Write it down.
- Now, select a couple of things on which you'll use the **5 Second Rule.** Commit to using the rule for at least a week. When you think of washing the dishes, calling someone, or *insert your chosen task*, count down from five to zero, and take action before you reach zero.

Common mistakes to avoid when conditioning your mind:

As you condition your mind to experience more positive emotions, avoid making the following mistakes:

- **Trying to implement too many changes at once:** Stick to one or two exercises for a month or so before trying any other exercises.
- **Starting too big:** Keep it small and make sure the exercises aren't too challenging. Remember, taking control of your emotions is a long-term game. It's a marathon, not a sprint.

To learn in more about how to create an exciting morning ritual, please consult my book, Wake Up Call: How to Take Control of Your Morning and Transform Your Life.

* * *

Action step

Refer to the corresponding section in the workbook and choose the emotion(s) you want to experience more of, (*Section III. How to change your emotions - 4. Conditioning your mind*).

15

CHANGING YOUR EMOTIONS BY CHANGING YOUR BEHAVIOR

> Action seems to follow feeling, but really action and feeling go together, and by regulating the action, which is under the more direct control of the will, we can indirectly regulate the feeling, which is not.

— WILLIAM JAMES, PHILOSOPHER AND PSYCHOLOGIST.

We've seen you can influence your emotions by using your body, mind, or words. We've also discussed how you can change your interpretations of thoughts or events to change your emotional state. Unfortunately, when negative emotions suddenly arise or are too strong, changing your body posture or using positive affirmation might not be enough. In fact, trying to replace a negative emotion by a more positive one often fails. You cannot always overcome depression by cheering up or counteract grief by deciding to just 'feel good.' Neither can you expect profound sadness to disappear by repeating the phrase/mantra, "I'm happy, I'm happy, I'm happy."

However, you can influence the way you feel by changing your behavior. As you alter your behavior, your feelings will change accordingly. It may happen almost immediately, as when you distract yourself from mild anger by performing a task. Or it may take weeks or even months while you deal with profound emotions such as intense grief or depression.

To start changing the way you feel, whenever you experience a negative emotion, ask yourself the following questions:

- "What causes that emotion?" and
- "What can I do about my present reality?"

After asking these questions, identify concrete actions you could take to change your emotional state.

Remember, by nature, emotions will fade as time passes. That is, unless you reinforce them by replaying the same situation over and over in your mind. Below are some real-world examples to help you better understand how it works:

Example 1:

If, after your boyfriend or girlfriend broke up with you, you keep remembering the good times you had together with sadness, it will take longer to get over the break-up. Although there is nothing wrong with feeling sad or remembering the past, if you want to move on, a better option is to avoid revisiting the past wherever possible. In this case, changing your behavior would be: do your best to stop revisiting the old memories.

Example 2:

If you constantly worry about an upcoming presentation at work, changing your behavior might be rehearsing your speech for hours. Doing this, you'll know the text so well you'll be able to perform well even under pressure. To give yourself an even better chance at success, you could also rehearse in front of your colleagues or friends.

Example 3:

If you've been resenting a particular friend for weeks because of something he said or did, changing your behavior might be having an honest talk with him and share your feelings. This will allow you to clear the air, clarify any misunderstandings, and avoid building up resentment. Oftentimes, we misinterpret events, or see things that aren't there.

Example 4:

Sometimes, you feel sad, angry, or even depressed, and can't do anything about it. In this instance, the best you can do is to avoid focusing on your feelings, and just let them be. Your job here is to do what you have to do and live your life until these emotions fade. Don't forget to practice letting go of negative emotions as they arise. As you learn to detach yourself from the negative emotions, it will help prevent them from growing and becoming more entrenched.

* * *

Action step

Using the workbook, let's do an exercise using an example from your life, (*Section III. How to change your emotions - 5. Changing your emotions by changing your behaviors*).

- Remember the last time you experience a negative emotion that lasted more than a couple of days.
- Now, think of what you did specifically to overcome this negative emotion (if anything).

- Then, ask yourself, "How could I have changed my behavior to influence my emotions positively?"

16

CHANGING YOUR EMOTIONS BY CHANGING YOUR ENVIRONMENT

You cannot always control your emotions. Certain events, such as a breakup, the loss of a loved one, or a severe disease, can trigger negative emotions.

However, you do have control over some events. Do you have daily life situations that affect your peace of mind? What if you could do something about them?

Sometimes, to reduce negative emotions you simply need to avoid putting yourself in the situations generating them in the first place. Perhaps, you watch too much TV, which makes you miserable. Or maybe, seeing your friends (seemingly) happy on Facebook makes you feel like a failure. Why not spend less time in such situations?

Real life example:

Facebook was making me unhappy and I felt like a failure. People in my field were killing it and my friends looked so happy (or so I thought). Not to mention the fact I was wasting hours of my time mindlessly scrolling through my newsfeed. To overcome this drain on my emotional 'bank', I drastically reduced the time I spent on Facebook. Ever since making the decision, I've been feeling better.

This example shows you that small changes can enhance your well-being. If you look at the things you do daily, you'll find activities or behaviors that don't support your happiness. Just removing one or two of these activities, or changing some of your behaviors, may noticeably improve your mood.

You may already know what you should do, but it's also possible you're unaware of the cost of some of your behaviors on your well-being.

Below, I've listed some examples of activities or behaviors that may rob you of your happiness. Ask yourself whether they're contributing to your overall sense of well-being:

- **Watching TV:** Although watching TV can be fun, it's also a passive activity which may not contribute much to your happiness.
- **Spending time on social media:** Social media is convenient and it allows you to keep in touch with your friends, but it can also be addictive. Facebook or Twitter can turn you into an addict craving the approval of others.
- **Hanging out with negative people:** People you hang out with have a tremendous influence on your emotional state. Positive people will lift you up and help you achieve your wildest dreams. Negative people will suck up your energy, demotivate you and destroy your potential. As Jim Rohn said, *"You are the average of the five people you spend the most time with."* Make sure you surround yourself with the right people.
- **Complaining and focusing on the negative:** Do you constantly see the negative side of things? Do you dwell on the past? If so, how does this affect your level of happiness?

- **Not finishing what you start:** Leaving tasks and projects unfinished in your personal and professional life can have a detrimental effect on your mood. Unfinished business clutters your mind. Feeling overwhelmed or demotivated, is a sign you may have too many 'open loops' in your life. Examples of 'open loops' are unfinished projects you've been procrastinating over, or avoiding people you need to talk to.

These are just a few examples. What about you? What activities or behaviors rob you of your happiness?

* * *

Action step

Design a more empowering environment by completing the corresponding exercises in the workbook, (*Section III. How to change your emotions - Changing your environment*).

Use the free workbook or take a pen and paper, and write down any activities you believe may negatively impact on your emotions. Then, for each activity, write down the consequence, (e.g. they make you feel guilty, they demotivate you, they erode your self-esteem, etc.).

17

SHORT-TERM AND LONG-TERM SOLUTIONS TO DEAL WITH NEGATIVE EMOTIONS

No other life-form on the planet knows negativity, only humans, just as no other life-form violates and poisons the Earth that sustains it. Have you ever seen an unhappy flower or a stressed oak tree? Have you come across a depressed dolphin, a frog that has a problem with self-esteem, a cat that cannot relax, or a bird that carries hatred and resentment? The only animals that may occasionally experience something akin to negativity or show signs of neurotic behavior are those that live in close contact with humans and so link into the human mind and its insanity.

— ECKHART TOLLE, THE POWER OF NOW.

In this section, I will provide you with a list of exercises or techniques you can use to better deal with negative emotions. No matter how much control you have over your mind, you'll still experience a whole bunch of negative emotions in the future, from mild frustration to depression. You'd better be prepared.

I've listed below some things you can do to deal with negative emotions and have included both long-term and short-term solutions.

1. Short-term solutions

The following techniques will help you manage negative emotions as they arise. Try them out, and keep the ones that work for you.

A. Change your emotional state

- **Distract yourself:** An emotion is only as strong as you allow it to be. Whenever you experience a negative feeling, instead of focusing on it, get busy right away. If you're angry about something, cross something off your to-do list. If possible, do something that requires your full attention.
- **Interrupt:** Do something silly or unusual to break the pattern. Shout, do a silly dance or speak with a strange voice.
- **Move:** Stand up, go for a walk, do push-ups, dance, or use a power posture. By changing your physiology, you can change the way you feel.
- **Listen to music:** Listening to your favorite music may shift your emotional state.
- **Shout:** Talk to yourself with a loud and authoritarian voice and give yourself a pep talk. Use your voice and words to change your emotions.

B. Take action

- **Do it anyway:** Leave your feeling alone and do what you have to do. Mature adults do what they have to do whether they feel like it or not.

- **Do something about it:** Your behavior indirectly changes your feelings. Ask yourself, "What action can I take in today to change the way I feel?" Then, go do it.

C. Become aware of your emotions

- **Write it down:** Take a pen and paper and write down what you worry about, why, and what you can do about it. Be as specific as possible.
- **Write down what happened:** Take a piece of paper and write down what exactly happened to generate the negative emotion. Don't write down your interpretation of it or the drama you created around it. Write down the raw facts. Now ask yourself, in the grand scheme of your life, is it really that big a deal?
- **Talk:** Have a discussion with a friend. You may be overreacting, making things worse than they are. Sometimes, all you need is a different perspective.
- **Remember a time when you felt good about yourself:** This can help you get back in that state and gain a new perspective. Ask yourself the following questions, "How did it feel?" "What was I thinking at the time?" "What was my outlook on life at the time?"
- **Let your emotion go:** Ask yourself, "Can I let that emotion go?" Then, allow yourself to release it.
- **Allow your emotions to be:** Stop trying to resist your emotions or to change them. Allow them to be what they are.
- **Embrace your emotion:** Stay with your emotions. Look at them as closely as possible while doing your best to remain detached. Become curious about them. What are they exactly at their core?

D. Just relax

- **Rest:** Take a nap or a break. When you're tired, you're more likely to experience negative emotions than when you are properly rested.
- **Breathe:** Breathe slowly to relax. The way you breathe affects your emotional state. Use breathing techniques to calm you down, or to give you more energy.
- **Relax:** Take a few minutes to relax your muscles. Start by relaxing your jaw, the tension around your eyes and the muscles on your face. Your body affects your emotions. As you relax your body, your mind also relaxes.
- **Bless your problems:** Thank your problems. Understand they are here for a reason and will serve you in some way.

2. Long-term solutions

The following techniques will help you manage your negative emotions long-term.

A. Analyze your negative emotions

- **Identify the story behind your emotions:** Take a pen and paper, and write down all the reasons why you have these emotions in the first place. What assumptions do you hold? How did you interpret what's happening to you? Now, see if you can let go of this particular story.
- **Write down your emotions in a journal:** Take a few minutes each day to write down how you felt. Look for recurrent patterns. Then, use affirmations, visualization, or a relevant exercise to help you overcome these emotions.

- **Practice mindfulness:** Observe your emotions throughout the day. Meditation will help you do this. Another way is simply to engage in an activity while being fully present. As you're doing this, observe what's going on in your mind.

B. Move away from negativity

- **Change environment:** If you're surrounded by negativity, change your environment. Move to a different place, or reduce the time you spend with negative friends.
- **Remove counterproductive activities:** Remove or reduce the time you spend on any activity not having a positive impact on your life. This could be reducing the time you spend watching TV or surfing the internet.

C. Condition your mind

- **Create daily rituals:** This will help you to experience more positive emotions. Meditate, exercise, repeat affirmations, create a gratitude journal, and so on. (The best time to deposit positive thoughts in your mind is right before going to sleep and first thing in the morning.)
- **Exercise:** Exercise regularly. Exercise improves your mood and is good for your emotional and physical health.

D. Increase your energy

The less energy you have, the more likely you are to experience negative emotions.

- **Improve your sleep:** Make sure you get enough sleep. If possible, go to bed and wake up at the same time every day.

- **Eat healthier food:** As the saying goes, "You are what you eat." Junk food will negatively impact your energy levels, so take steps to improve your diet.
- **Rest:** Take regular naps, or take a few minutes to relax
- **Breathe:** Learn to breathe properly.

E. Ask for help

- **Consult a professional:** if you have deep emotional issues such as extreme low self-esteem or depression, it might be wise to consult a professional.

* * *

Action step

Write down one short-term and one long-term technique you want to use. Ask yourself, "Among the items on the list, what is the one technique that will best help me deal with negative emotions?" (*Section III. How to change your emotions - Short term solutions/long term solutions*).

PART IV

HOW TO USE YOUR EMOTIONS TO GROW

I suggest to you that every situation, every moment, provides the opportunity for self-growth and development of your character. Reality keeps bringing us circumstances —sometimes I picture them as waves breaking on the shore—and we have the chance to keep merging with that reality to fit ourselves to it, to dive into those waves.

— DAVID K. REYNOLDS, AUTHOR OF CONSTRUCTIVE LIVING.

We've seen what emotions are, how they are formed, and how you can reprogram your mind to experience more positive ones. Now, let's see how you can use your emotions as a tool for personal growth.

Most people underestimate how useful emotions can be. They never truly realize they can use their emotions to grow.

Think of it this way. Your emotions send you a message. They tell you that your current interpretation of reality is biased. The problem is never reality, but the way you interpret it. Never forget, you have the power to find meaning and joy even in the worse situations.

For instance, Alice Sommer had every reason in the world to feel hopeless. She was imprisoned in a concentration camp during WWII and didn't know how long she had left to live. She, nevertheless, found joy. As she recalls:

> *I was always laughing. We were lying on the floor with my son, and he saw me laughing. How can a child not laugh when the mother laughs?*
>
> — ALICE SOMMER

Nick Vujicic believed he would never be happy. After all, he was born with no arms or legs. As he said in one of the lectures he gave at a school,

> What kind of husband am I gonna be if I can't even hold my wife's hand?
>
> — NICK VUJICIC

Under these circumstances, nobody would have blamed him if he had remained bitter all his life. However, he overcame his challenges and today, in addition to being a successful motivational speaker, he's a happy husband and father of two.

These two examples show us we can overcome even the most challenging situations. They show us negative emotions don't last forever. Challenging times in our life are often the events that allow us to grow as human beings. Even a complete nervous breakdown can serve as a wake-up call for people.

In this section, you'll learn how emotions work and how you can use them to grow, while simultaneously reducing the emotional suffering they create.

18

HOW EMOTIONS CAN GUIDE YOU IN THE RIGHT DIRECTION

Emotions come and go and, ultimately, can't define you. But it doesn't mean they don't have a role to play. They can foster your personal growth by reminding you of what you already know: you need to make changes in your life. The more you ignore your emotions, the louder they will become. It starts with a small voice, a gut feeling or an intuitive knowledge. As you dismiss this sign, it gets louder. Keep ignoring your emotions, and your body will begin to talk in the same way as you experience physical pain.

For instance, let's say you feel an emotion you identify as 'stress.' This tells you to make changes in your life. It could involve moving away from a stressful situation, improving the situation, or changing how you interpret it. One thing is sure, you need to do something about it. If you keep ignoring stress or the stressor, it may result in severe health issues.

The bottom line is, your emotions send you a message. In the same way that physical pain tells you something is wrong with your body, emotional suffering tells you something is wrong with your mind.

The power of self-awareness

Self-awareness is one of the most important components of your personal growth. Without it, you can't do much to change your life, since you can't change a problem unless you realize it exists.

So, what is self-awareness? Self-awareness is your ability to observe objectively your thoughts, emotions, and behaviors without adding your own interpretation or story to it.

Above or below the line?

In *The 15 Commitments of Conscious Leadership*, Jim Dethmer and Diana Chapman introduced a very simple yet powerful model to help increase self-awareness. This model is extremely simple: a single line. The authors argue that, at any time, you're either above or below the line. When you're above the line, you're open, curious and willing to learn, but when you're below the line, you want to be correct and, as a result, you tend to be defensive and closed to new ideas. Put it simply, when you're above the line you're conscious, when you're below the line you're unconscious.

Whether you are above or below the line depends on your emotional state. When you sense a threat to your physical survival or to your ego, you fall below the line and try to protect yourself in order for you (or your ego) to survive. Conversely, when you operate above the line, you're in a positive state of mind. Your creativity, innovation, and collaboration are at their best, resulting in enhanced performance.

Your ability to recognize when you fall below the line largely determines how well you can control your emotional state. You can't change an emotion if you don't notice its presence. This is what being 'aware' or 'conscious' means. Below are some examples of 'above the line' and 'below the line' behaviors.

Above the line, you are:

- Curious
- Listening consciously
- Feeling emotions
- Discussing without being argumentative
- Appreciating
- Taking responsibility, and
- Questioning your beliefs.

Below the line, you are:

- Clinging to an opinion
- Finding fault
- Arguing
- Rationalizing and justifying
- Gossiping
- Enrolling others to affirm your beliefs, and
- Attacking the messenger.

Fear vs. love

Another simple model you can use is the **Fear vs. Love Model**. Throughout your day, you either act out of fear or out of love. You act out of fear when your focus is on getting something, be it other people's approval or attention, money or power. On the other hand, when you act out of love, your main focus is on giving, be it your time, money, love, or attention. You want to share and improve the lives of people around you, not for your own interest, but simply for the sake of it.

While your actions can simultaneously reflect your desire to give and to receive, one or other of these components is generally more pronounced. To master your emotions, you must learn to identify whether you're acting out of love or fear. For instance, look at one of your major life goals. Is it a fear-based goal or a love-based goal? Are you trying to give and contribute to the world, or are you trying to take from it?

For instance, let's say you want to become an actor. Some of the reasons for that could be the following:

1. Making money
2. Being famous
3. Proving to your parents and friends you're good enough
4. Entertaining people
5. Expressing yourself

The first three examples are usually fear-based behaviors: you want to fill a void within yourself and demonstrate how good you are. The final two examples are love-based behaviors that stress a desire to express your gift to the world.

As we discuss in greater depth how different emotions work, keep in mind these two models: **above/below the line** and **fear-based vs. loved based** actions.

Note that throughout your day you often alternate between love-based behaviors and fear-based behaviors. For instance, you may be absorbed by a task that helps people and make you feel complete. In this moment, you don't need anything. Five minutes later you may imagine how proud your father will be once you finally earn a promotion. In this moment, you're no longer feeling complete. Instead, you are trying to get something, (in this situation, your father's approval).

Start noticing the underlying motivations behind your actions. As you do so, you'll begin to realize you spend a considerable amount of time trying to earn other people's approval, whether they be your colleague, your boss, your parents, or your partner. Notice this, and ask yourself what you can do to move from 'wanting to get' to 'wanting to give.'

Now, with these two models in mind, let's see how you can bring more awareness to the emotions you experience in your day-to-day life.

19

RECORDING YOUR EMOTIONS

The first step to improve the way you feel is to become more aware of the emotions you experience on a regular basis. Before you can generate more positive emotions, you must first determine your starting point.

To shed a light on the emotions you're experiencing in your daily life, I invite you to record your emotions for an entire week. Use a notebook or the downloadable worksheet to do so. Spend a couple of minutes each day to record how you feel and rate yourself on a scale of 1 to 10, one being the worst you can feel, and ten being the best you can feel. At the end of the week, give yourself an overall score and answer the following questions:

- What negative emotions did you experience?

- What caused these emotions? What are the hard facts?

- Did you have specific thoughts that lead you to feel that way? Did external events trigger these negative emotions? Did you lack sleep? Did you become ill? Were you in an accident?

- What really happened? (Not in your mind, but in the physical world)

- What was your interpretation of the facts?

- What would you need to believe to feel that way?

  • Are your beliefs accurate?
  • Could you have felt better by interpreting thoughts or events differently?

- How did you return to your neutral state?

  • What happened exactly? Did you change your thoughts? Did you take action on things you were avoiding doing? Did it just happen naturally?

- What could you have done to avoid or reduce these negative emotions?

Concrete example:

Let's say you record your emotions for a week and notice that you were mildly depressed for a couple of days. Here is what it could look like:

What caused this emotion?

I was asked to do a task at work and felt unable or incompetent to complete it.

What really happened?

I was asked to complete a task and I did it.

What was your interpretation of the facts?

  • I felt like I was incompetent and everybody in the office but me could do the task.

- I felt as though I should have been able to do the task well.
- I felt as though everybody was judging me.

What would you need to believe to feel that way?

I would need to believe:

- I am incompetent.
- Being incompetent is unacceptable.
- I should have been able to do that task.
- Everyone is judging me.

Are your beliefs true?

Are you really incompetent?

- Maybe I'm biased and I judged myself too harshly.

Is being incompetent unacceptable?

- No. The fact is, I cannot always be competent at everything.

Should you be able to do that task?

- I haven't much experience performing similar tasks and there was no way I could do it without asking for help.

Is it true that everyone judging you?

- Some people may judge me, but that's probably not true of everyone. It's also possible nobody really cares. After all, they have their own issues to deal with. And what if nobody noticed? Or perhaps, I did okay and the negativity is all in my mind.

How did you return to your neutral state?

I realized it was actually no big deal. I asked a colleague whether I did the task correctly. He helped me and gave me some advice. He also recommended some good books to help improve my skills.

What could you have done differently to avoid or reduce this negative emotion?

I could have asked someone to help me instead of trying to do everything on my own.

As you go through this process, you'll notice what causes you to experience negative emotions. You'll be able to identify self-defeating behaviors and overcome them using daily conditioning and affirmation.

Additional tip:

Remember to write down how you feel each day using a dedicated journal. This will help you detach yourself from your emotions as you realize ups and downs are a normal part of living.

* * *

Action step

Record your emotions using the workbook, (*Section IV. How to use your emotions to grow - Record your emotions*).

20

NOT BEING GOOD ENOUGH

> ❝ When I won the Oscar, I thought it was a fluke. I thought everybody would find out, and they'd take it back. They'd come to my house, knocking on the door, 'Excuse me, we meant to give that to someone else. That was going to Meryl Streep.
>
> — JODIE FOSTER

> ❝ You think, 'Why would anyone want to see me again in a movie? And I don't know how to act anyway, so why am I doing this?'.
>
> — MERYL STREEP

Do you feel as though you aren't good enough? Guess what! You're not the only one. The other day I wrote the following to a fellow blogger:

"There are a lot of topics I could write about but there are already so many books out there. Sometimes, I'm like 'What's the point?'"

He replied:

"I know the feeling of, 'What's the point?' Everything worth saying has already been said. And who am I to write about it anyway? What have I achieved so far? Ah, well... I guess it's natural. Good to know that we're not the only ones struggling."

Whether or not you're aware of it, millions of people feel the same way. The feeling of 'not being good enough' alone must have killed more dreams than anything else. And who has never felt that way? Here is a (non-exhaustive) list of how I felt in my life:

- I'm not a good enough writer
- I'm not charismatic enough
- I'm not competent enough
- I'm not confident enough
- I'm not courageous enough
- I'm not disciplined enough
- I'm not good enough at public speaking
- I'm not handsome enough
- I'm not inspiring enough
- I'm not interesting enough
- I'm not making enough money
- I'm not muscular enough
- I'm not patient enough
- I'm not perseverant enough
- I'm not pro-active enough
- I'm not productive enough
- I'm not smart enough
- I'm not taking enough action
- I'm not tough enough
- I'm not working hard enough
- My English isn't good enough
- My Japanese isn't good enough, and
- My memory isn't good enough.

And I could go on.

People who feel they aren't good enough tend to have low self-esteem. They focus on what they *aren't* good at while filtering out all the things they *are* good at. Try complimenting them and all you'll hear is, "It's no big deal." Worse, they may even think you're being polite, or trying to manipulate them. These people have a hard time accepting compliments. Instead of a simple thank you, they return the compliment, or downplay their role.

Perhaps, you're acting the same way? See if you do one of the following things when receiving a compliment:

1. Dismiss the whole thing as being no big deal: "Anybody could have done it."
2. Talk about all the things you did wrong while explaining what you could have done better.
3. Try to return the compliment: "Thank you. I think you did a fantastic job, too."

Notice your inability to accept a compliment hundred percent in the three cases above.

You may not only brush off your accomplishments, but also magnify every single of your failure to reinforce the case you aren't worthy. You keep a long list of your failures, unwilling to let go of them as they fit your story. Who would you be if you were no longer the man or woman who's never good enough? As strange as it may seem, there's something scary about that. At least, the certainty of not being good enough gives you some comfort.

Imagine what would happen if you release the hold you have on your story, try something you've always wanted to do, and fail. What you suspected for a long time would become true: you aren't good enough. Or worse, what would happen if you were to succeed? How would that fit into your story?

Remember, your brain is biased towards negativity. Adding your own bias will certainly not help you feel good about yourself. The fact is, you do most things well. Although a lack of experience, interest, or talent may explain why you aren't doing as well as you would like to in certain areas, it has nothing to do with you not being 'good' enough.

How to use the feeling of not being good enough to grow

Not feeling good enough is a sign of low self-esteem. Many people experience low self-esteem in various degrees. I certainly do. For some, every single thing they do is insufficient. For others, they feel inadequate only in certain situations or areas of their life. Wherever you are on the self-esteem spectrum, you can probably benefit from a boost in your self-esteem.

Identifying what triggers your feelings of inadequacy

The first step is to find out what triggers these feelings. What thoughts are you identifying with? Which areas of your life are concerned?

Take a few minutes to write down the following:

- The situations in which you feel like you aren't good enough, and
- The thoughts you identify with (your story).

Keeping track of your accomplishments

The second step is to keep track of your accomplishments. Not feeling good enough often results from the biased view you hold about yourself. You focus on your shortcomings, failing to acknowledge your successes. People with healthy self-esteem tend to look at themselves in a more objective way, acknowledging both their shortcomings *and* their strengths.

To improve your self-esteem, start acknowledging all the things you're doing well. The following exercises will help you do that.

Exercise 1 - Create a win log

One of the best ways to acknowledge your accomplishments is to write them down. For this exercise, I encourage you to use your dedicated notebook.

1. First, write down everything you've accomplished in your life. Come up with a list of fifty things. If you run out of things, write smaller accomplishments. This will help you realize how much you've already accomplished.

2. At the end of each day, write down all the things you've accomplished that day. It can be simple things such as:

- I woke up on time
- I exercised, and
- I ate a healthy breakfast.

Try to come up with five to ten things each day.

Exercise 2- Fill up your self-esteem jar

An alternative is to write down each thing you've accomplished on separate pieces of paper and put them into a jar. Here are a few recommendations to ensure you make the most out of this exercise:

- Make sure your jar (or any other container you use) is in a visible location. The best location is probably on your desk, the second-best location is your bedroom.
- Select a container you like. Choose a design you're fond of. It's all about your self-esteem so anything that makes you feel good is advisable. Make sure it is transparent so that you can see it filling up.

- Give it a positive name, (e.g. my self-esteem jar, declaration of love to myself etc.).
- Write your accomplishment on a paper you love. For instance, use different colors so that when the jar fills up, it creates something pleasant to the eye. One idea would be to use origami paper.
- Write with your favorite pen.

The idea is to show more respect towards yourself by acknowledging your multiple accomplishments.

Exercise 3 - Create a positive journal

You can also create a journal to write down every compliment you received that day. Your colleague told you your shoes look nice, write it down. Your friend complimented your hair, write it down. Your boss told you how well you did at a task, write it down as well. Don't question the sincerity of these compliments. Always assume they are genuine. The idea is to train your mind to focus on the positive things that happen in your life—they are happening whether or not you acknowledge them. Here is how to make the most of that exercise:

- Buy a notebook you like.
- Personalize it: Add stickers, draw something, add pictures or use different colors. Don't want to do any of this stuff? That's fine as well. It's *your* journal.
- Keep it with you: Carry it with you and look for new compliments to add to your amazing collection (optional).
- Review it every day: Go through old entries and mentally thank people who complimented you. You can say, "Thank you *insert name*, I love you." Feel free to read the old entries in the morning, in the evening or both (or whenever you feel like it). It's up to you.

Again, this is *your* journal. These are just suggestions. Whatever works for *you*.

Learning to accept compliments

Chances are you have difficulties accepting compliments. Do the following sentences look familiar:

- It's never a big deal.
- Everybody could have done it.
- It's because 'so and so' helped you.
- I could have done it better.

Here is a great reason why you should accept compliments: because **the person who made the compliment wants you to receive it, not to flush it down the toilets!** Imagine you just gave a gift to someone. How would you feel if that person, after opening the box, dropped the gift to the floor, stepped on it and threw it away? You wouldn't like it, would you? Sadly, that's what we often do when we receive a compliment. When we refuse to accept a compliment, we are disrespecting the person who went out of their way to deliver it. Wouldn't you want your compliment to be accepted wholeheartedly?

Exercise 1 - Accept compliments

This simple exercise will help you accept a compliment. Whenever someone compliments you, say the following:

Thank you *insert the person's name*.

That's it. There is nothing simpler. No, "Thank you, but...", "Thank you, you too," or "It wasn't a big deal." Simply say, "Thank you."

Here is how to make the most of that exercise:

- Say thank you out loud and clearly. You may discover you

have the tendency to repress your feelings and end up saying thank you almost mechanically. In fact, you may realize you've never really said, "Thank you," with all your heart.

- Let it sink in: Before you start a new sentence, give space for the feeling of gratitude to express itself. Don't downplay the compliment or explain why you're worthy (or unworthy) of it.
- Tell it the way you feel it: Show your appreciation by telling the person who complimented you how you feel. You may experience resistance. Many of us have difficulties expressing gratitude, because our pride prevents us from doing so. After all, we're strong and don't need anybody's help or compliments, do we? We don't want to feel vulnerable. If you experience resistance and find the exercise difficult, recognize this is normal.

Your ability to accept a compliment can be a good indicator of your level of self-esteem. Practice accepting compliments and allow yourself to feel vulnerable. Accepting you're worthy of compliments will help you boost your self-esteem.

Exercise 2 – The appreciation game

The purpose of this game is to learn to appreciate things in yourself you didn't previously acknowledge (or like). It will work well if you have a partner you can play the game with on a regular basis. Tell your partner three things you appreciate in them and ask them to do the same. Be as specific as possible and don't worry about coming up with big things. Here are some examples:

- I appreciate that you prepared breakfast this morning even though you were in a rush.
- I appreciate that you picked up the kids today.

- I appreciate the way you always listen to my problems after work.

To go further:

Self-esteem is a complex topic. It affects a lot of people and is often misunderstood. Overcoming low self-esteem takes time and effort. If you regularly feel you aren't good enough, I encourage you to refer to the following books. If, upon reading these books, you realize you have severe and chronic self-esteem issues, you may want to consult a specialist.

- *The Six Pillars of Self-Esteem,* by Nathaniel Branden, PhD.
- *Breaking the Chain of Low Self-Esteem,* by Marilyn Sorensen, PhD.
- *Low Self-Esteem: Misunderstood & Diagnosed: Why You May Not Find the Help You Need,* by Marilyn Sorensen, PhD.

Below is a brief summary of some of the main ideas in each book:

In his book, *The Six Pillars of Self-Esteem,* Nathaniel Branden, identified six practices (or pillars) of self-esteem you can work on to develop a healthier self-esteem:

1. **Living consciously:** In Nathaniel Branden's words, "to live consciously means to seek to be aware of everything that bears on our actions, purposes, value, and goals—to the best of our ability, whatever that ability may be—and to behave in accordance with that which we see and know."

2. **Self-acceptance:** Is choosing to value yourself, to treat yourself with respect and to stand up for your right to exist. Self-acceptance is the basis upon which self-esteem develops.

3. **Self-responsibility:** Is realizing no one is coming to save you and you are responsible for your life. It is accepting that you are

responsible for your choices and actions. You are responsible for how you use your time, and for your happiness. Because only *you* can change your life.

4. Self-assertiveness: Means, honoring your wants, needs, and values and seeking appropriate forms of their expression in reality.

5. Living purposefully: Is to use your powers to achieve the goals you have selected. In other words, it's your ability to set and achieve goals in every area of your life.

6. Personal integrity: Is behaving in a way that matches your ideals, convictions, and beliefs. It's when you can look at yourself in the mirror and know you're doing the right thing.

In *Breaking the Chain of Low Self-Esteem*, Marilyn Sorensen provides a great overview of what self-esteem is and how it works. The author explains that low self-esteem stems from the negative perception you hold of yourself—a perception that is largely, if not entirely, based on your negative interpretations of past experiences. This distorted perception of reality leads you to experience fear and anxiety. Your family environment may have played a big part. Perhaps, your parents have repeatedly put you down, making you feel as though nothing you did was ever good enough.

You may now firmly believe you are less worthy than others. As a result, you filter everything based on this negative image of yourself. It's as if you were looking at reality through tinted glasses; glasses that discard praise and compliments, remembering only criticisms.

The examples in her books will help you understand how self-esteem issues manifest in real life. In addition, Ms Sorensen provides dozens of practical exercises to help you become more aware of your self-esteem issues along with the tools to develop a healthier self-esteem.

* * *

Action step

Refer to the exercises in the corresponding section of the workbook, (*Section IV. How to use your emotions to grow - Not being good enough*).

21

BEING DEFENSIVE

> Our love of being right is best understood as our fear of being wrong.

— KATHRYN SCHULZ, JOURNALIST AND AUTHOR.

Do you constantly justify yourself? Are you offended whenever someone insults you or disrespects you?

There are very specific reasons why you get defensive. By becoming conscious of these reasons, you'll learn a lot about yourself and be able to let go of that desire to defend yourself. First, let's see why you get defensive.

Why you get defensive

The need to defend yourself stems from your desire to protect your story (or your ego). Every time your ego is threatened, you are triggered and feel the need to defend it. I believe there are three main reasons why you are triggered.

1. There is part of truth in what you were told.
2. You believe there is part of truth in what you were told.
3. A core belief you hold has been attacked.

Note that because we all have different stories, what triggers you might not trigger someone else.

1. There is part of truth in what you were told

Someone mentioned something that is true about you and it hurts. For instance, he or she may accuse you of procrastinating on a certain project. Your inability to accept that truth is the reason you become defensive. When that topic is brought up, it triggers emotional reactions such as anger, denial or self-criticism.

2. You believe there is part of truth in what you were told

You were told something you believe to be true and feel hurt. In this case, the criticisms you received may be unfounded. Yet, you still feel hurt. Why is that? It's because what you were told confirms the disempowering beliefs you hold about yourself. For instance, let's say you believe you aren't good enough. This belief pushes you to work harder than anybody else. Now, how would you feel if someone accused you of being lazy? You would feel offended, wouldn't you? However, that wouldn't be because you're actually lazy, but because of *your belief* that you should work harder.

3. One of your core beliefs has been attacked

Someone directly or indirectly attacks one of your core beliefs, and you feel the need to defend yourself. This could be a religious belief, a political belief, or a more general belief about the world or yourself. The more attached you are to this belief, the stronger your emotional reaction will be. Here is a great example:

Because they believed Donald Trump was evil, some Liberals had strong emotional reactions after he was elected president. Some shouted and even became violent. On the other hand, many Conservatives were delighted by Trump's victory.

How come people can react so differently to the same event? This is because of their core beliefs. Both Democrats and Republicans strongly identify with their political beliefs. This led hardcore Democrats to burst into tears and hardcore Republicans to rejoice.

Whenever a belief you're strongly attached to is attacked or challenged, you'll experience an emotional reaction. The deeper the belief is, the stronger the emotional reaction will be when it is attacked. An extreme example would be someone ready to kill anybody who dares to criticize his or her religion.

How to use this emotion to grow

Look at the situations that triggers you. Whenever you feel offended, ask yourself why. What belief led you to defend yourself? Can you let go of this belief? And is this belief really true?

By doing this, you'll learn a great deal about yourself. You'll be able to let go of beliefs that aren't serving you well, and you'll realize that, in most cases, you don't even need to defend yourself.

Action step

Refer to the exercises in the corresponding section of the workbook, (*Section IV. How to use your emotions to grow - Getting defensive*).

Whenever you become defensive, remember to ask yourself the following questions:

- What am I trying to protect here?
- Can I let go of that belief?
- What would I be without that belief?

22

STRESS AND WORRY

66 Within every worry is an opportunity for positive action. In every lie, there is a kernel of truth. Behind every neurotic symptom is the misdirected desire to live fully and well.

— DAVID K. REYNOLDS, CONSTRUCTIVE LIVING.

Have you ever wondered what stress is and why you experience it?

Most people believe a situation can be stressful. The truth is, stress doesn't exist outside of yourself and, therefore, no situation can be said to be stressful in itself. Yet, my guess is you experience stress on a regular basis. And probably more often than you would like to.

Stress alone is responsible for tens of thousands of deaths every year. Stress does more harm than many diseases, and leaves countless families grieving the loss of a loved one. This is why it is essential you take active steps towards reducing your stress levels.

Taking responsibility for your stress

Stress is something you have some control over and, therefore, must take responsibility for. The more you take responsibility for it, the better you'll be able to reduce it.

Stress happens for various reasons and manifests in numerous situations. The traffic jam on your way to work, a business presentation, tensions with your boss, or frequent disputes with your spouse, all constitute potential sources of stress. There are two ways you can reduce stress:

- By avoiding situations you perceive as stressful, and
- By becoming better at dealing with stressful situations.

We'll see how you can use these methods to reduce your stress levels.

How you can use stress to grow

Exercise - Make a list of your major sources of stress

Let's look at specific situations that are sources of stress for you. Using the workbook, write down what causes the most stress in your typical week. Come up with at least ten things.

Reframing stress

Emotions arise as a result of your interpretation of events. The mere fact you experience stress (or any other emotion) means you've added your own interpretation to what is happening. Otherwise, you would have a stress-free life.

Now, look at your list of stressful situations. For each situation ask yourself the following questions:

- Is that situation stressful in itself?
- What do I need to believe to experience stress in that specific situation?
- What would I need to believe to reduce or remove stress in that particular situation?

Let's say you're stuck in a traffic jam and you find it stressful.

Is that situation stressful in itself?

No, not necessarily. The traffic jam exists and there is nothing wrong with it, *per se.*

What would I need to believe to experience stress in that specific situation?

I would need to believe:

- There shouldn't be any traffic jams, and therefore, something is wrong.
- The traffic jam is a stressful event in itself.
- I should be where I need to go, instead of being stuck in traffic.
- I can do something about it.

What would I need to believe to reduce/remove stress in that particular situation?

I would need to believe that:

- A traffic jam is a normal event like anything else.
- I don't necessarily have to experience stress just because I'm stuck in traffic.
- I'm here caught in a traffic jam and I don't need to be there (wherever I want to go), for a while.
- I can't do anything about it, so I might as well enjoy it, or at least don't stress over it.

Dealing with worry

Worry differs from stress as it isn't the result of something you experience in the present, but a concern you have regarding events from the past or events that may happen in the future. You experience *stress* when you face a stressful situation in the present moment.

For instance, a stressful situation would be being stuck in a traffic jam or having your boss yell at you. Worrying would be remembering (past) or anticipating/imagining these stressful situations (future). Interestingly, most of your worries are unnecessary for the following reasons:

- They happened in the past and there's absolutely nothing you can do about them, and/or
- They may happen in the future and you can't control the future.

Exercise - Make a list of your worries

Make a list of things you worry about (past or future). They may be similar to the things you wrote in the previous exercise. Examples of things you may worry about are:

- Your health
- Your financial situations
- Your work
- Your relationships, and/or
- Your family.

Now, write at least ten things you tend to worry about in a typical week.

Sorting out your worries

Constant worry results from trying to control events over which you have no control. When you do so, you create unnecessary stress in your life. To deal with stress and overcome chronic worries more effectively, it is essential you learn to sort out worries. An effective way to do this is to separate the things you have control over from the things you have no control over. You can divide your worries into three separate categories:

1. Things you have control over
2. Things you have some control over, and
3. Things you have no control over whatsoever.

1. Things you have control over:

This category includes things such as your actions and behaviors. For instance, you can choose what to say and how to say it. You can also decide what actions you'll take to achieve your goals.

2. Things you have some control over:

There are things you have only limited control over such as a competition or a job interview. You can't be absolutely certain you'll win a tennis match but you do have some control over its outcome. For instance, you can choose to train harder or hire a great coach. Similarly, you can prepare for a job interview by conducting extensive research about the company you apply to, or by doing a mock interview. You don't, however, have absolute control over the outcome of the interview.

3. Things you have no control over:

Unfortunately, there are also many things you have no control over. These are things such as the weather, the economy, or traffic jams.

Exercise - Sort out your worries

Look at your list of stressful situations. Next to each item, put C (control), SC (Some control), or NC (No control). This simple act of sorting out your worries already helps reduce them. As you identify things you have no control over, you can let go of your urge to worry.

Now, for things you have (some) control over, write down what you could do about it. What concrete actions could you take to alleviate them?

For things you have no control over, can you let go of your need to control them and, instead, accept them?

Taking one hundred percent responsibility for your stress and worries

What if you had more control over your worries than you believe? Look at the situations you have no control over and ask yourself, "If I had control over them, what would I do? What would it look like? And how could I prevent them from happening?"

Often, you'll realize you have some control over these situations. This can be by changing, reframing or eliminating them from your life.

Let's say you identified traffic jams as something you have no control over. This sounds reasonable. Once you're caught in the traffic jam, you can't do much about it. But, could you do things differently? For instance, could you leave home earlier or take a different route?

What about reframing the situation? Instead of escaping the situation mentally, you could choose to be fully present by making traffic jams a productive part of your day. You could then make the most of it by listening to audiobooks. Imagine how much you could learn if you listened to audiobooks every working day for an entire year.

Go over your list and look for things you have no control over. Write down what you could do to change, reframe or eliminate these events.

* * *

Action step

Refer to the exercises in the corresponding section of the workbook, (*Section IV. How to use your emotions to grow - Stress / Worry*).

23

CARING WHAT PEOPLE THINK OF YOU

> How on earth can another's thought about you harm you? It is your thought about his thought that harms. Change your thought.
>
> — VERNON HOWARD, THE POWER OF YOUR SUPERMIND.

Are you overly self-conscious? In this section, I'll explain why you care so much what people think of you and what you can do alleviate the situation.

You are the most important person in the world

First, realize you are the most important person in the world. If you don't believe me, remember the last time you felt intense pain. Perhaps, it was toothache or surgery, or maybe, you broke your leg in an accident. What were you thinking back then? Were you concerned about the famine in Africa? Did you worry about innocent people being killed in wars in the Middle East?

No.

The only thing you wanted is for the pain to go away. This is because you are the most important person in the world. Since you must live with yourself 24/7, it is normal to be concerned about your own mental and physical well-being.

You have to realize the same goes for every other human on the planet. For me, you're not the most important person in the world —I am. And, from their perspective, so are your close friends, family members and colleagues.

Because you live with yourself 24/7 you incorrectly assume, often unconsciously, people think about you significantly more often than they actually do. In fact, for the most part, people do not care about you. While it may sound depressing, it's actually liberating. It means you don't have to worry so much about what people think of you.

As the famous saying goes:

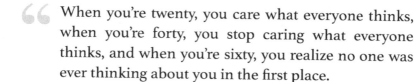 When you're twenty, you care what everyone thinks, when you're forty, you stop caring what everyone thinks, and when you're sixty, you realize no one was ever thinking about you in the first place.

While you keep track of all your mistakes and awkward moments, nobody else does. People are simply too busy worrying about themselves. In short, people don't:

- Keep track of your past failures
- Read everything you post on social media
- Remember your awkward moments
- Think of you (very often), or
- Care about you as much as you care about yourself.

Not everybody will love you

You care what other people think of you because you want them to approve of you. You assume the best way to do that is to avoid making waves. As a result, you may spend your whole life trying to be the perfect person, hoping to be loved.

However, it usually doesn't work. No matter how great you are, some people won't like you. You may try to 'fix' the image people have of you, but that won't work either. People will still see you the way they want to, because of their own values and beliefs.

Thus, if you base your self-worth on what people think of you, you'll always be at the mercy of the approval of others. What will happen if they suddenly disapprove of you? Unfortunately, no amount of external approval will compensate for a lack of self-approval.

By trying so hard to be loved by everybody, you risk living a dull life in which you're unable to express your personality. You'll end up mimicking your friends, pleasing everybody around you, but forgetting to please the most important person in the world—*you*.

What people think of you is none of your business

You're not responsible for people's thoughts. In fact, what people think of you is none of your business. Your job is to express your personality the best way you can, while having the purest intent possible. In short, your responsibility is to do your best to be your true self. Then, people may or may not like you, and either way is fine. Remember, the most influential people such as presidents and statesmen and women are often hated by millions.

Therefore, don't make it your personal mission to change people's image of you. People are entitled to their beliefs and values, and they have the right to dislike you. They are free to interpret your actions and behaviors through their own filter. Part of your personal growth is to accept you don't have to be liked by everybody, and finally, you can be yourself.

How to use this emotion to grow

Being overly self-conscious means:

1. You have a distorted view of the way people perceive you, and
2. You are attached to a self-image you want to protect.

To stop being so self-conscious you must address these two points.

1. Change your interpretation of the way people perceive you

To care less about what people think of you, it is essential for you to redefine your relationships with other people. This entails realizing that:

- In general, people don't care about you, and
- You don't care about people.

Exercise 1 - Realizing people don't care

This exercise will help you understand at a deep level, most people are not really concern about you.

- Choose one person you know. It might be a friend, an acquaintance, or a colleague.
- Ask yourself how often you think about that person in your daily life.
- Now, put yourself in the shoes of that person. How much do you imagine he or she thinks about you during an average day? How much does he or she keep track of what

you do or say? What do you think he or she is worrying about right now?

- Repeat this process with at least two more people.

As you do this exercise, you'll probably realize other people are simply too busy to think of you often. After all, they live with themselves 24/7. In their own eyes, they are the most important person in the world. Not you. And this is only to be expected.

Exercise 2 - Realizing you do not care

You're not that concern about other people either. The following exercise will make you realize this.

- Go through your day and try to remember all the people you met or interacted with. It might be the waitress or the customers in the restaurant you lunched in, the people you saw on the street, and so on.
- Ask yourself how much you thought about these people prior to this exercise. You probably didn't think of them at all, did you?

As you can see, you don't really have time to worry about other people. Most of the time you are concerned only about yourself. It's not to say you have no compassion or are a selfish jerk. You're merely being human.

Stop being overly attached to your self-image

If you are overly self-conscious, chances are you worry too much about the way people perceive you. Perhaps you want their approval or are afraid they will judge you. It is essential you learn to let go of this self-image.

Exercise - Letting go of your self-image

- Write down all the things you're afraid to be judged on: Maybe you worry about your look, or you're afraid of saying something silly.
- Write down why you care: What is the issue here? What image are you trying to protect? Do people believe you're smart and you're afraid you can't live up to this image? Are you afraid of being rejected as a result of saying something wrong?

This exercise will bring awareness to the things you're worrying about and will help you address them. In addition, don't forget to complete the exercises mentioned in the section, 'Letting go of your emotions.'

Finally, remember people will always interpret your words and actions based on *their* values and beliefs. Therefore, to let your personality shine, you have no choice but to allow them to see you whatever way they wish.

* * *

Action step

Refer to the exercises in the corresponding section of the workbook, (*Section IV. How to use your emotions to grow - Caring what people think of you*).

24

RESENTMENT

" Even if we can't love our enemies, lest at least love ourselves. Let's love ourselves so much that we won't permit our enemies to control our happiness, our health, and our looks.

— DALE CARNEGIE, HOW TO STOP WORRYING, AND
START LIVING.

When you resent people, you're angry at them because they didn't behave the way you wanted them to. Maybe they broke their promises, or perhaps they didn't give you what you expected from them. Perhaps you believed they owed you something, but they failed to deliver?

Resentment often builds up when you fail to communicate effectively with the people you resent. That is, when you didn't tell them you felt hurt, or didn't communicate your needs and wants, assuming they would naturally cater to them. It can also grow when you did express your feelings but can't let go of them and forgive. As Nelson Mandela once said, *"Resentment is like drinking poison and then hoping it will kill your enemies."* It just doesn't work.

Resenting people

As with any other emotion, resentment will grow in intensity following the formula: interpretation + identification + repetition = strong emotions.

You can resent someone for years for a rather insignificant event based on:

- Your interpretation of the event
- Your identification with the story you're telling yourself about it, and/or
- The number of times you replay the event in your mind.

Let's say one of your friends 'betrayed you' by not inviting you to a party. In your mind, your friend truly betrayed you and you deeply resent him for it. You can't stop thinking, "How could he do that to me?" The thought consumes you for weeks and you decide to cut ties with him. Months later you're still resenting him. Notice that the event in itself isn't upsetting. What creates resentment is your interpretation of the event.

Now, is it possible that your interpretation was wrong? What if your friend assumed you wouldn't like the party? What if he thought you were too busy? Sure, he should have at least invited you, but nobody is perfect. If you'd put aside your interpretation and confronted him at the time, maybe things would have turned out differently.

The danger of letting resentment build up

Often, what adds fuel to the fire is your inability or unwillingness to confront the people you resent. Instead of this, you keep revisiting in your mind what (you think) happened. As a result, your resentment grows stronger as time passes. This is especially true if you regularly interact with people you resent.

How to use resentment to grow

Resentment occurs when you are unable to forgive and move on with your life. It is the result of being attached to what was in the past instead of focusing on what could be in the future. When you experience resentment, you are provided with an opportunity to learn how to forgive and let go and, more importantly, how to love yourself.

Resentment is here to tell you that you must love yourself and value your peace of mind more than anything else. Your peace of mind must become more important than being right, taking revenge, or hating someone else. In short, moving beyond resentment is making a declaration of love to yourself so you can move on, while, at the same time, showing compassion to others.

Loving yourself

Paraphrasing Nelson Mandela's words, resentment is a poison you consented to drink. Resentment are the weeds you allow to grow in your garden. When you experience resentment, you believe that something you were legitimately entitled to was unjustly taken from you. For instance, it could be someone else's trust, respect, or love. As a result, you feel as though you've been attacked personally.

Resentment will subsist as long as your need for being right and getting even is more important than your peace of mind. It will keep growing as long as you keep feeding the emotion with thoughts of resentment. And it will remain as long as you repress it. That's why it's important you make your peace of mind a priority and learn to forgive others as well as yourself.

Loving others

Your ability to release resentment is linked to your level of compassion. The more compassionate you are, the easier it will be to let go of resentment. One important thing to understand is that people always act based on their level of consciousness (or unconsciousness). You may wish someone had acted differently toward you, but if he or she didn't, it's probably because he or she was unable to do so.

Thus, rather than saying people are good or bad, it is more accurate to say they are either conscious or unconscious. When they do terrible things to you, it's often because of their lack of consciousness, or the negative emotional state they were in at the time.

Sadly, most people are deeply conditioned. Their upbringing leads them to act in a certain way. People often act the same way as their parents, which is why you often hear of people who've been abused by their parents, becoming, in turn, abusive with their children.

As Eckhart Tolle wrote in the Power of Now:

> The mind, conditioned as it is by the past, always seeks to re-create what it knows and is familiar with. Even if it is painful, at least it is familiar. The mind always adheres to the known. The unknown is

dangerous because it has no control over it. That's why the mind dislikes and ignores the present moment.

In short, the nature of the (unconscious) human mind is to cling to old patterns and recreate them. Look at your family history and you'll probably notice these patterns. You'll see how people are conditioned. This shows how difficult it is for people to break free from set patterns.

I used to resent my mother for being overly protective. I blamed her for not encouraging me to grow, but instead, her actions made me weaker than I already was. Perhaps, it was one of the reasons I embarked on a personal development journey. However, I realized she didn't have any bad intentions. She simply meant well and did the best she could.

The point is, people do what they can, with what they have, based on who they are and how much they've been conditioned. They make tons of mistakes as well. We all do. It's part of being human.

One of the most ridiculous things we try to do as human beings is to want to change the past. What happened in the past was supposed to happen. Because it did happen. Now, the question is, what are you going to do about it?

How to deal with resentment

To start letting go of resentment, we'll discuss the importance of:

1. Changing/reevaluating your interpretation
2. Confronting the situation
3. Forgiving (breaking free from identification), and
4. Forgetting (stopping the repetition).

Resentment results from your interpretation of something that happened to you. This interpretation leads you to feel betrayed and to experience anger, or even a desire for revenge. By revisiting the scene in your mind, you allow resentment to build and, because you avoid confronting the situation or person at the root of your resentment, the emotion continues to grow.

To prevent resentment from building, it is necessary for you to reevaluate your interpretation of what happened, while confronting the situation or person you resent. After doing this, you must be willing to forgive and release your resentment. Finally, you must choose to forget. This entails not replaying the scene in your mind over and over again.

1. Changing/reevaluating your interpretation

To put things into perspective, it is important for you to look at your interpretation of what happened. Might you have over-dramatized the situation? Is it possible you misinterpreted something? Ask yourself, what exactly happened? After you remove your interpretation, only the hard facts will remain. Looking at what really happened may provide you with valuable insights, allowing you to replace your current interpretation with a more empowering one.

2. Confronting the situation

If your resentment is directed toward people, perhaps you need to have an honest discussion with them and share how you feel.

Often, resentment builds up when you don't share your feelings with the person you resent. This is often due to fear: fear of appearing vulnerable, fear of hurting the other person, or fear of negatively impacting your relationship with that person. If you can't talk to that person directly, an alternative it to write a letter. Even if you don't send it, the simple act of writing the letter may help you release some of your resentment.

3. Forgiving

Now you've found a channel to express yourself, you can start to forgive. You've looked at the hard facts and reevaluated your interpretation. If needed, you had an honest discussion with the person you resent. You did what you had to do, and now you can let it go.

Think of the negative consequences created by resentment. Write down how it affects your happiness and peace of mind. Remember, resentment is the result of your attachment to the past. Forgiveness is simply reconnecting with the only thing that is real, the present, while forgetting about what isn't real, the past. Then, release it. Imagine how your life would be and how you would feel once you've let go of the resentment. Do it right now. Then, let go. Forgive.

Remember, forgiving is an act of self-love. **You forgive not just because you have compassion, but because you value your happiness more than anything else.** As you forgive, you let go of the attachment to your story, and you distance yourself from the thoughts related to it. To let go of resentment, you can use the five-step process introduced in the section, 'Letting go of your emotions.'

4. Forgetting

Finally, forget. Forgetting is when you stop entertaining thoughts of resentment and simply move on. When such thoughts arise, let them go. Over time they will lose their power.

* * *

Action step

Complete the exercise in the corresponding section of the workbook, (*Section IV. How to use your emotions to grow - Resentment*).

25
___

JEALOUSY

When you experience jealousy, you desire something someone else has, but you don't currently have. We all feel jealous from time to time, and this is not something you should blame yourself for. In this section, I will explain how jealousy works and provide you with some solutions to deal with it.

How to use jealousy to grow

Jealousy stems from the belief you aren't good enough. It comes from a place of lack and scarcity. You want something someone else has, believing that it would fulfill you. Alternatively, you're afraid of losing something or someone you believe is yours.

Jealousy can help you find what you really want

Jealousy can let you know you're on the wrong path and can help you find out what you really want. For instance, in her book *Quiet,* Susan Cain explained she would often feel jealous of her friends who were writers or psychologists. Interestingly, even though she was a lawyer at the time, she didn't feel jealous of successful lawyers—as her lawyer friends often did. This led her to realize she wasn't made to be a lawyer. As a result, she changed her career and became a writer.

I had a similar experience. While I was a consultant, I didn't envy or look up to successful people in my company. On the other hand, on my personal development journey, I became envious of successful personal development bloggers and YouTubers. I felt particularly jealous of two such people when I realized they were doing exactly what I wanted to do. I imagined how amazing it would be to help other people and make a contribution to society while studying and growing along the way. This is why I created a blog and started writing books. As you can see, jealousy, when properly used, can be beneficial.

Exercise - Identify who you are jealous of

Write down who you are jealous of. Now, what does it say about you and what you want from life?

Jealousy can signal a scarcity mindset

In other situations, jealousy may indicate you're operating under a scarcity mindset. Let me give you another example from my personal life. When I see bestselling writers, I sometimes become jealous. I feel as though they are stealing my piece of the pie, and I deserve success as much as they do. I'm not proud of this feeling, but I don't blame myself for having it, either.

This feeling of jealousy stems from the belief there is only a certain amount of success available out there. Thus, every time someone has a little success, they are stealing your piece of the action. Interestingly, this is often not the case. If anything, for writers the opposite is true. The more a writer can cooperate with other writers, the better chances he or she has to succeed. A writer who tries to do everything on his or her own is likely to fail. This is not limited to writers, of course. Shifting your mindset from one of competition to one of cooperation can help you move from a feeling of scarcity to a feeling of abundance.

Nowadays, when I see other writers having success, I remind myself what great news it is. After all, if they can do it, so can I. And the more successful my fellow writers become, the more they are in the position to help me in the future. This also works the other way around. The more I help other writers to succeed, the more they'll be able to help me in the future. As Zig Ziglar said, *"You can have everything in life you want, if you will just help other people get what they want."* Remember, what other people can do, you can do as well. Remember also, success is not a limited resource.

Exercise - Cooperate rather than competing

Think of a time in the past when you felt jealous of someone else's accomplishments. Now, ask yourself why you felt that way. Then, ask yourself:

- What would it be like to support the person?
- How could I cooperate with the person?
- Why is that person's success good for me?

Jealousy may tell you to solve self-esteem issues

Perhaps you're afraid your boyfriend or girlfriend may cheat on you, or leave you for someone else. This usually comes from the belief you aren't good enough, and you need your boyfriend or girlfriend to 'complete' you. Unfortunately (or fortunately), the same way you can't control what people think of you or how they behave, you can't control your loved one's thoughts or behaviors either. Often, the very same desire to control your partner is what pushes them further away. While feeling jealous from time to time is normal, if you're excessively jealous, it is essential you look within you. Your insecurities and fears usually come from a lack of self-esteem and from the fear that you can't or won't be loved.

Jealousy may lead to some of the following behaviors:

- Trying to control your partner: You may check your partner's phone or emails or prevent them from going out to see their friends.
- Testing your partner to see whether he or she loves you: You may expect your partner to behave in a certain way and when he or she doesn't, you feel betrayed. This stems from the belief that you shouldn't have to tell your partner what you want or need. He or she should be able to guess.
- Imagining things that aren't there: You make up all sorts of stories in your mind by extrapolating facts.

I invite you to refer to the section, 'Not being good enough,' to discover how to develop a healthier self-esteem.

Jealousy may signal you to stop comparing yourself with others

> One kind of lingering discontent, shared by millions, is the notion that others are happier than they are. I assure you, they are not. If you could only see the secret sorrows of those whose smiles and activities seem to indicate happiness. If you could only see how fervently they wish to be somewhere else, doing something different, being someone other than who they are.

Jealousy often results from comparison with others. It is important to realize this type of comparison is generally as counterproductive as it is biased. Indeed, you seldom compare apples to apples. You look at some of your friends' successes, but you fail to realize this is only part of the picture. While they may seem happy and successful on the surface, it is quite possible they are unhappy or even depressed. The point is, rather than assuming your friends are happier than you are, it is better to assume that *you* are as happy as *they* are.

Also, guard against looking only at areas in which your friends seem to have it better than you. Perhaps, you focus on the fact they're making more money than you, or have a partner while you are single. Or perhaps you envy them for some of their natural strengths and abilities. The problem here is you fail to make an 'apple to apple' comparison. You dismiss your own strengths or qualities which make you feel as though you're not as good as they are.

Even worse, you may often compare yourself with several other people. You look at areas in which they are successful and then you look at your own life to see how well you compare. Of course, not very well. How could you compete with the combined strengths of several people! Can you see how biased and unrealistic this type of comparison is? Yet, this is what many of us do, albeit unconsciously.

The bottom line is, if you feel jealous, it may be because you engage in this type of unfair comparison. Instead, why not compare your 'today's' self with your 'yesterday's' self. After all, the only thing you can do is to try to be better than you were yesterday, last month or last year. Because we all start with different circumstances, skills and personalities, there is no such thing as a fair comparison.

Exercise - Compare apples to apples

This exercise will help you compare yourself to others more fairly.

Select someone you often compare yourself with. Write down all the things you're doing better than that person.

* * *

Action step

Refer to the exercises in the corresponding section of the workbook, (*Section IV. How to use your emotions to grow - Jealousy*).

26

DEPRESSION

> The hardest thing about depression is that it is addictive. It begins to feel uncomfortable not to be depressed. You feel guilty for feeling happy.
>
> — PETE WENTZ, MUSICIAN.

Non-clinical depression occurs when you're not where you want to be in life, you have lost any hope to ever be, and can't accept it. This might happen after a tragic event in your life or more progressively as some aspects of your life slowly fall apart. Depression results from feeling hopeless in one or several areas of your life. Here are some examples:

- You lost your job and have no hope of finding a new one to match your expectations.
- You're sick and have no hope to recover as well as you would like to.
- You are divorced from your partner and can only see your kids once in a while.

- You have little hope of finding a suitable partner.
- You're in so much debt that it seems as though you'll never get out of it.
- You suffered a bereavement.

While the events above are tragic, depression can also be created out of more 'ordinary,' less severe events. For instance, some people may spend so much time dwelling on the past or worrying about the future they eventually become depressed. This may happen even though no significant events have occurred in their lives.

It is essential to remind yourself that depression, like other emotional states, is neither good nor bad, it just is. You are not your depression. You existed before it, you exist during it and, all things being equal, you will exist after it.

Depression is an active process

While it may seem as though depression is happening to you, it is, in fact, created by the negative thoughts you identified with. Thus, you do have some responsibility in creating your depression. Does it mean you should feel guilty or beat yourself up for being depressed? Of course, not! Never. In fact, you should never beat yourself up for any of the emotions you feel. That would be pointless. What it means, however, is that, because you've played a part in creating your current emotional state, you also have the power to get out of it. And that's great news, right?

Remember Dr. David K. Reynolds' first-hand experience with depression? He wrote the following:

> Depression can be created by sitting slouched in a chair, shoulders hunched, head hanging down. Repeat these words over and over: 'There's nothing

anybody can do. No one can help. It's hopeless. I'm helpless. I give up.' Shake your head, sigh, cry. In general, act depressed and the genuine feeling will follow in time.

— DAVID K. REYNOLDS, CONSTRUCTIVE LIVING.

David K. Reynolds' depression was entirely self-created. It was an active process that involved adopting a certain body language, repeating certain words, and having certain thoughts. He had to act in a certain way to become depressed.

The good news is that because you have the power to 'create' depression, you also have the power to climb out of it. However, in a negative state such as depression, ignoring negative thoughts and replacing them with more positive ones can be extremely challenging. Even if you try to think positive thoughts of gratitude, joy, or happiness, at first, they will seem to have no power.

But you may experience other negative emotions such as anger for instance. You may ignore your anger at first. Your friends may even encourage you to do so—they would rather see you quiet and depressed, than angry. However, sometimes anger may help you move up the emotional ladder and overcome depression. Keep in mind, any emotions other than depression can help and learn to embrace whatever emotional state seems to give you more energy, and therefore provide more power to move up the emotional ladder.

David K. Reynolds also suggests that feelings fluctuate over time even with depressed people. He wrote, "*In the deepest depression there are ripples and waves of somewhat lighter moods.*" You can use moments when you feel slightly better to take whatever action may be beneficial to you at that time.

How to use depression to grow

Depression is a sign you've lost touch with reality. Have you noticed that human beings are one of the few species on earth that have the ability to become depressed. This is because they are the only ones who can get lost in their mind and become enslaved by negative thoughts and disempowering stories.

Depression is a sign that you need to move away from your mind —by letting go of your worries about the past/future or your interpretation of the present situation—and reconnect to the present moment. It can be a powerful invitation to let go of the identity you've been clinging to for so many years. This identity is what led you to believe you should be doing certain things, making a certain amount of money, adopting a certain lifestyle, or developing a certain social status.

Depression invites you to reconnect with your body and emotions while getting out of your head. After all, didn't your mind create the depression in the first place? Some people who experience severe grief, sadness, or depression like to keep themselves busy to avoid thinking. When depressed, more thinking is seldom the solution. You rarely see people getting out of depression by using their mind.

Therefore, instead of thinking, you want to reconnect with your body. Exercising is a great way to do this and has been shown to be effective in improving your mood. (For additional information refer to the section "The benefits of exercising")

In some rare cases, severe depression can lead people to separate from their mind. When this happens, their story suddenly drops. Apparently, this is what happened to Eckhart Tolle as he recalls in his book, *The Power of Now*. He had a sudden awakening and his mind stopped. Here is what he wrote about his experience:

 This withdrawal must have been so complete that

this false, suffering self immediately collapsed, just as if a plug had been pulled out of an inflatable toy.

— ECKHART TOLLE.

In summary, depression tells you to let go of your ego and reconnect with reality. It invites you to get out of your mind, which can only recall the past or anticipate the future, and live more in the present. Severe depression may require the help of a professional, but for milder depression here are some mediating strategies:

Exercise - Reconnect with your body and your emotions

To overcome depression, it is essential for you to escape your mind. It's easier to 'feel' your way out of depression than to 'think' your way out of it. I would venture to say that most people spend over ninety percent of their lives in their mind. They have only rare moments of lucidity when they are fully aware and present. For instance, they don't listen to people, but they:

- Judge and interpret what they say
- Anticipate what they'll say next, and/or
- Get lost in their thoughts.

All these things happen at the 'mind' level and show how people are not fully present. Because they either live in the past or in the future (i.e. in their mind), they experience a number of negative emotions. Below are some of the things you can do to reconnect with your body and your emotions:

Exercise: As previously discussed, exercising is a great way to calm your mind and connect with your body, and it has a positive effect on your mood.

Meditate: Meditation is an effective way to observe your mind and stop identifying with your thoughts so heavily. Meditation is simply a tool to help you reconnect with reality by observing thoughts, emotions, and sensations instead of getting lost in your mind.

Activity: Getting busy allows you to avoid excessive thinking. Instead of feeding your depression with constant negative thoughts, concentrate your attention on something else.

Focus on others: As mentioned in Dale Carnegie's book, *How to Stop Worrying and Start Living*, Alfred Adler used to say to his melancholia patients, *"You can be cured in fourteen days if you follow this prescription. Try to think every day how you can please someone."* Whether or not it is accurate, focusing on others can certainly help you forget about your own issues and focus on something more positive.

Unfortunately, when you feel depressed you won't want to do any of these things. However, as you start moving and start keeping yourself busy, your situation will gradually improve, and it will become easier and easier. Thus, it is important to take things just one step at a time.

* * *

Action step

Refer to the exercises in the corresponding section of the workbook, (*Section IV. How to use your emotions to grow - Depression*).

27
___

FEAR/DISCOMFORT

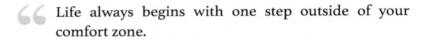 Life always begins with one step outside of your comfort zone.

— SHANNON L. ALDER, INSPIRATIONAL AUTHOR.

Whenever we try something new, we experience anxiety. We are afraid of the unknown. This is why we like to maintain our daily routine and stay within our comfort zones. From our brain's point of view, this makes perfect sense. If our current habits allow us to be safe and avoid any potential threat to our survival (or the survival of our ego) why bother changing them? This explains why we often keep the same routine, or have the same thoughts over and over. It is also why we may experience a lot of internal resistance when trying to change ourselves.

Thus, when we try to move beyond our comfort zones, we experience fear and distress. Now, do we want to stay in the same place most of our lives and avoid taking any risks, or do we want to pursue our dreams and see what we are truly capable of becoming? We have to remember, most of our fears are a threat only to our ego, not to our survival. Generally, they aren't physical threats, but imaginary ones. If we play it safe we risk missing out on life, and we may regret it later.

Below are common fears you may experience:

Fear of rejection: You're afraid of being rejected. This may be physical rejection from a specific group, but it is generally more subtle. For instance, you may be afraid of:

- Making a comment people could disapprove of
- Asking someone out and being turned down, or
- Sharing your work and being criticized for it.

Fear of failure: You're afraid of failing. This usually comes from the deepest fear of not being good enough, i.e. you are afraid of being ridiculed and believe that failure will erode your self-esteem.

Fear of loss: Human beings have an aversion to loss, which is why we are often more motivated to prevent a loss than to secure a gain.

Fear of disturbing: You're afraid of disturbing people. Perhaps due to the belief you're not important enough. As a result, you may feel reluctant to affirm yourself for fear of appearing selfish.

Fear of success: You're afraid of success. You may worry you won't be able to sustain it with all the added pressure on your shoulders.

How to use fear to grow

The fear of doing something new is often a sign you should go ahead and do it anyway. This indicates a great opportunity for personal growth. Fear, as with any other emotion, only exists in your mind. This is why we often realize what a fool we've been after we've completed something we were initially wary of starting.

People who end up reaching their wildest goals often do so because they are willing to leave their comfort zone. Over time, they learn to be comfortable with the uncomfortable. Picture one thing you were once afraid to do, that is now no big deal for you. For instance, I bet you were scared the first time you drove, or on your first day at work. Now, didn't you get used to it?

The truth is, people have the formidable ability to learn. The key is to grow accustomed to experiencing discomfort once in a while. By not facing your fears on a regular basis, you will greatly limit your potential for development. Staying inside your comfort zone can also erode your sense of self-esteem as, in the back of your mind, you know you're not doing what you're supposed to do.

There is a law in nature: things either grow or die. The same goes for humans beings. When humans don't move beyond their comfort zone, they start dying inside. Don't let that happen to you. As Benjamin Franklin said, "*Some people die at twenty-five and aren't buried until seventy-five.*" Make sure 'some people' doesn't include *you*!

Taking action

The first step to move out of your comfort zone is to realize even the most successful people on earth feel fear. Courage is not the absence of fear, it is taking action *despite* the fear. Courage is realizing fear is not going to go away and doing what you want to do anyway. **Without fear, there is no courage.** As you face fear on a regular basis, you cultivate courage and turn it into a habit.

You don't need to avoid fear or numb yourself to it before you can take action. Instead, you must accept the fact that fear won't go away and get used to it. Then, you must decide to take action.

Exercise - Move out of your comfort zone

To start moving out of your comfort zone, you can ask yourself, "What is the one thing I should be doing, but fear has made me procrastinate over?" Once you do that one thing, you'll likely experience a sense of pride and of being alive. This is a sign you're on the right track. See it as the reward your brain gives you for moving beyond your comfort zone.

Action step

Refer to the exercises in the corresponding section of the workbook, (*Section IV. How to use your emotions to grow - Fear/Discomfort*).

28

PROCRASTINATION

> Only put off until tomorrow what you are willing to
> die having left undone.

— PABLO PICASSO

Procrastination is largely an emotional issue. While there are effective techniques to deal with procrastination, for the most part, learning to manage your emotions properly is the key to overcoming your tendency towards delayed action.

Why you procrastinate

There are different reasons why people procrastinate. Below are some of them:

- The task is boring
- The task is seen as unimportant
- The task is too challenging (or perceived as such)
- You're afraid you'll do a poor job, and/or

- You are habitually lazy.

Imagine if the task was lots of fun, perceived as important, and so easy you couldn't fail, would you procrastinate?

I believe fear is the main reason people procrastinate. Afraid they'll do a poor job, people would rather put off a task. While they may convince themselves that the task is not urgent or important, or that they are tired, often, the truth is they are scared.

Note that procrastination isn't in itself a sign you are lazy, or that something is wrong with you. We all procrastinate. However, if you regularly suffer from procrastination, it may indicate you either have self-esteem issues, or you lack self-discipline.

How to use procrastination to grow

Procrastination might suggest you believe too much in what your mind is telling you. Instead of being the master of your mind, you've become its slave. This comes at the cost of:

- not living the life you want
- not accomplishing your dreams, and
- experiencing low self-esteem, guilt and unhappiness.

Remember, when your mind tells you, "You're tired. Let's rest," or "Let's do it tomorrow," it's not an order. You don't have to follow it. You aren't your emotions. Neither are you your mind. No matter what thought may cross your mind, you can choose to either accept it, or ignore it.

Now I would like to share a 16-step process to overcome procrastination. Don't worry, it's not as complicated as it might first appear.

How to Crush Procrastination in 16 Simple Steps

1. Understand what's hidden behind procrastination.

The first step is to understand why you procrastinate. As we've discussed previously, there are specific reasons behind procrastination. Usually, it has to do with fear, and the mind tells you the best way to avoid fear is simply to do nothing. In other words, to procrastinate. Another reason you procrastinate is because the task is difficult. You want to avoid pain as much as possible and maximize pleasure. This is how your brain works. You may also procrastinate because you lack motivation. This happens when the task you work on isn't part of a bigger vision that excites you. If you lack motivation, ask yourself why. Then, consider the following solutions:

- Delegate the task
- Eliminate the task
- Reframe the way you perceive the task to make it part of a bigger (and more exciting) vision
- Restructure the task so that it becomes easier, and/or
- Just get started (see step 13).

Spend time identifying all the reasons behind your procrastination. Be honest with yourself.

2. Remind yourself of the cost of procrastination

Procrastination is not a minor issue and comes with severe consequences.

- The direct consequence of procrastination is that you'll

achieve far less than you could during your time spent on earth.

- The indirect consequence of procrastination is that you may feel bad about yourself. You may blame yourself for not doing what you know you should be doing, which erodes your self-esteem and creates unnecessary worries.

Exercise - the cost of procrastination

Now, take a sheet of paper and write down what procrastination costs you.

How does it affect your peace of mind? Your self-esteem? Your ability to achieve your dreams? The more you're sick and tired of procrastination, the more likely you will be to actually do something about it.

3. Uncover your story

The third step to overcome procrastination is to identify the story behind it. What are you telling yourself when you feel the urge to procrastinate? What thoughts cross your mind? What excuses do you use? Some common excuses are:

- I'm too tired
- I'll do it tomorrow
- I'll do a poor job, and/or
- It's not really important.

Let's address some of these excuses right away

I'm too tired

While that may be true, you must realize you're not your mind. You don't need to listen to your mind. Navy SEAL, David Goggins, uses the forty percent rule. This rule states that, even when you think you can't take it anymore, you're using only forty percent of your brain's capacity. The bottom line is you have great reserves of energy you can tap into when you feel tired. Therefore, working two hours on your side business after work isn't going to kill you.

I'll do a poor job

If you schedule a task for today, it means you believe you can do it. Thus, the fear of doing a poor job isn't the issue here. After all, if you think you'll do a poor job today, what makes you think you'll do a better job tomorrow? You most likely won't. That's just a story you're telling yourself.

I'll do it tomorrow

Doing it tomorrow might not be a big deal. However, if you can't discipline yourself to finish today's tasks, what are the chances you will design your ideal life in the future? Remember, disciplining yourself to complete the task in front of you is, ultimately, what will allow you to create your future life. Time, effort, and self-discipline are required to create anything of value in your life.

It's not really important

Even if that is true, not completing a task you scheduled creates an open loop. Then, somewhere in the back of your mind you know that you still have to complete that task. If you keep putting off tasks, you'll soon start losing motivation. At some point, you may even end up feeling stuck without knowing why.

Exercise - Write down your excuses

Start becoming aware of all the excuses you come up with. Write them down, then, address them one by one. They control you because you let them. Commit to addressing them.

4. Rewrite your story

Look at your excuses. Are you too tired? Do you lack time? Are you trying to do everything perfectly? Now you've identified your story, create a new more empowering story to neutralize your old excuses. See the examples below:

- I don't have time for that → I find and make time for whatever I'm committed to.
- I'm too tired → I have control over my mind and I have more energy that I imagine. When I schedule a task, I complete it.

Then, create affirmations or mantras around your new story. Repeat them to yourself every morning and throughout the day until they become part of your identity. Remember, procrastination is a habit. You want to reprogram your mind and implement a new habit: the habit of working on the tasks you schedule whether you feel like it or not. (For more, refer to the section, 'Conditioning your mind.')

5. Clarify your 'why'

Procrastination is often due to a lack of motivation. When you're excited about a goal, you don't run away from it, do you? No. You can't wait to work on it!

Look at the tasks you regularly procrastinate over. Why is that? How can you make these tasks part of your vision to make you feel more motivated? Can you adjust these tasks? Can you learn something from these tasks? Can you envision yourself feeling proud of yourself as you complete these tasks?

The stronger your reason, your 'why,' the easier it will be for you to overcome your tendency to procrastinate.

6. Identify the ways you distract yourself

The next step is to notice all the ways you distract yourself. What are your own ways to procrastinate? Is it going for a walk? Watching videos on YouTube? Drinking coffee? Or perhaps, reading books on how to overcome procrastination?

Unless you're aware of all the ways procrastination manifests in your life, you'll have a hard time overcoming it.

Exercise - make a list of all the ways you procrastinate

Take a couple of minutes to write down all the way you procrastinate using the free workbook.

7. Stay with the urge

As you feel the urge to *insert your distraction here*, stay with the emotion. How do you feel? Allow yourself to feel the emotion. Don't judge yourself. Don't blame yourself. Just accept what is. As you do so, you'll gain more control of your mind, (refer to the chapter on 'Letting go of your emotions,' for more information)

8. Record everything you do

To assess your productivity and gather insights on ways you procrastinate, record everything you do in a notebook. Do it for one week. Each time you switch from one activity to another, write it down. Make sure you write how much time you spend on each task.

By the end of the week, you'll know how much time you spend doing 'real' work and how much time you spend distracting yourself. Be careful, you might be shocked.

9. Set a clear intent behind everything you do

Before working on a task, make sure you know exactly what needs to be done. Ask yourself, what am I trying to accomplish here? What will the end result look like? This way, you'll avoid giving your mind room to create excuses.

10. Prepare your environment

Your mind doesn't like what's difficult. It wants things to be easy. Thus, make sure you remove any friction or obstacle so you can work on your task immediately. For instance:

* If you want to run, have your running gear ready next to your bed so you can go run right after you wake up, (after a full warm-up first, of course).
* For computer-related tasks, remove all distractions from your desk and make sure you can access all the files you need immediately.

11. Start small

Instead of putting a lot of pressure on yourself, why not start small? Rather than writing two pages of your manuscript, maybe you can write one paragraph. Rather than exercising for one hour, why not start with five minutes? Making your tasks smaller will help you overcome procrastination. Not only that, but it will also allow you to build momentum. So, whenever you have an option, make sure you start small to reduce the pressure.

12. Create quick wins

Facing daunting tasks every day will set you up for failure and kill your motivation. Learn to chunk down your tasks and set small milestones, ones you can achieve easily. This will:

- Allow you to form the habit of completing your tasks one hundred percent
- Increase your self-esteem as you accumulate quick wins, and
- Reduce the urge you have to procrastinate.

Set small goals every day and accomplish them consistently for a few weeks. By doing so, you will increase your self-esteem and be better equipped to complete challenging tasks in the future. Remember, getting things done is a habit, and as with any other habit, it can be practiced and learned.

13. Just get started

Often, when you start working on a task, you'll enter what is called 'the flow' and things become effortless. In these instances, you become so focused on your task motivation will no longer be an issue.

The best way to enter a 'flow state' is by getting started. To make it easier, decide to work on a task for only five minutes and see what happens. Remove any pressure or desire to perform well and give yourself permission to do a poor job. You'll often end up working on the task for a lot longer than originally planned. Notice that the more attention your task requires, the more likely you are to enter the flow quickly.

In addition, you can use the **5-Second Rule** introduced by Mel Robbins in her book, *The 5 Second Rule*. This rule states that you only have a 5-second window to take action before your mind talks you out of it. (For more on the 5 Second Rule, refer to the section, 'Conditioning your mind.')

14. Create daily habits to support you

If you tend to procrastinate on important tasks, commit to working on them first thing in the morning. For instance, if you want to write a book, start writing every morning. Start small. For instance, set a tiny goal of writing fifty words a day, and do it every morning. As you maintain this schedule, you'll develop a writing habit and make procrastination less likely.

15. Use visualization

You can also use visualization to help you overcome procrastination. Below are two specific ways to do so:

1. Visualize yourself doing the task: See yourself turning on the computer, opening the file and writing. Imagine yourself putting on your running shoes and going for a run. This type of visualization has been shown to increase the likelihood you work on the task. Try it out.
2. Visualize yourself having completed the task: How would you feel once the task is done? Liberated? Happy? Proud? Now, feel as you would feel if you had completed your task. By doing so, you'll experience a boost of motivation that will encourage you to work on your task.

16. Build accountability

If you have a hard time completing a task, you might need some accountability. When I'm likely to procrastinate, I like to send a message to a friend and tell him I will complete a certain task by a specific date.

Another way to build accountability is to have an accountability partner you communicate with on a regular basis. You could talk to him or her once a week and share your list of goals. You could look at the important tasks you'll likely to put off and set a specific deadline for each one. Then, you could send an email to your accountability partner to let him or her know when you completed a task.

If you follow this 16-step process, you should be able to overcome or, at least, significantly reduce your tendency to procrastinate.

* * *

Action step

Follow the 16-step process using the corresponding section of the workbook, (*Section IV. How to use your emotions to grow - Procrastination*).

29

LACK OF MOTIVATION

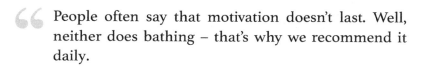 People often say that motivation doesn't last. Well, neither does bathing – that's why we recommend it daily.

— ZIG ZIGLAR, SALESMAN AND MOTIVATIONAL SPEAKER.

Lacking motivation is usually a sign that you don't have a compelling vision to pursue. People who have an exciting vision seldom lack motivation. While they may experience setbacks along the way and feel frustrated or even mildly depressed, they tend to bounce back quickly by reminding themselves of their vision.

Lack of motivation is also a sign you're not 'following your bliss.' It shows there is a misalignment between what you do and who you are. The word 'enthusiastic' comes from Greek and means, 'filled with the divine.' If you lack enthusiasm, you're probably out of touch with the essence of who you are.

I've never heard of a noble prize winner retiring early because he or she was bored. In fact, most of them will work until the day they die. This is because they have a clear purpose. Similarly, I've never seen billionaires selling their companies to retire on a tropical island. They may have tried but quickly realize how boring their lives have become.

The point is, you don't inherently lack motivation, you're just not doing what you're supposed to do. You haven't stretched yourself enough and haven't created a vision that inspires you. Perhaps, you're stuck at the same dead-end job that bores you to tears. Or maybe you're at your current job for the money, or to fulfill your parents' wishes. Then, it's no wonder you lack motivation. Fortunately, you can get your motivation back.

How to use motivation (or lack thereof) to grow

A lack of motivation says you need to design a life that is more in line with who you are. It entails having a deep knowledge of your strengths, personality, and preferences, while making sure you leverage them on a day-to-day basis.

Knowing your strengths

When you spend most of your day doing things you suck at, how do you feel? Probably, not very motivated. Sadly, many people are stuck in jobs that do not allow them to use their strengths. As a result, they keep struggling, and keep wondering if their fate is to suffer the same way for the next forty years. I've experienced first-hand the difference between working at a job you suck at, and working on something you love and feel good at. I can attest that the level of motivation and energy you have when you do what feels right to you can be extraordinary.

Have you noticed you tend to like the things you're good at? You may not necessarily enjoy the task in itself but receiving positive feedback gives you a sense of pride and make you feel good about yourself. Now, if you were constantly reminded what a poor job you're doing, would you still love that same task?

The point is, there are things you are good at as well as things you enjoy doing. Once you identify the tasks you're good at and spend as much time as you can on them, you'll feel more motivated. You may even find yourself enjoying tasks you would never have imagined simply because you're good at them.

To be able to focus on your strengths, you may have to redesign your current job description, change jobs within the same company, or change your career altogether. Remember, if every second of the day is a struggle, you're probably not doing what you're supposed to do. You have strengths and your job is to find them.

Knowing your personality

This is somewhat related to the previous point since your personality partially determines what you're good at. For instance, if you're an introvert, you're likely to take different career choices than if you were an extrovert. You may prefer spending most of your time alone or in small groups and may stay away from jobs that require you to interact with clients all day long. You may find yourself performing better in a quiet environment.

Your core values will also affect your level of motivation. Perhaps, independence is vital for you. If so, being self-employed might be a better idea than having a 9-to-5 job. Or maybe you like novelty and want to be learning constantly. If so, doing the same repetitive job might not bring you much satisfaction.

Knowing what motivates you

Sometimes you lack motivation because you set a goal in a way that doesn't inspire you. While the goal may be something you genuinely want, the way you frame it, or work on it is just not motivating you.

Let's say you want to lose weight. If none of the reasons behind your goal touch you at an emotional level, you won't feel motivated, and will have a hard time achieving your goal. Thus, your job is to find out what losing weight will do for *you*. Ask yourself *why* you want to lose weight. Keep asking yourself why until you find something that resonates with you at an emotional level. Remember, you seldom want to lose weight because it's the 'right thing' to do. You want to lose weight because it will make you feel a certain way. This is the meaning you give to losing weight, and you must get it right if you want to succeed.

Now, you can also ask yourself why you *don't want* to lose weight. It may help you uncover the reasons why you're struggling. If you overeat because it makes you feel good, you need to ask why is that? Is it a habit? Is it because you're stressed? Is it because of your environment? Is it a way to escape from something?

Knowing why you're doing something is important. Once you have a strong why, who knows what you can accomplish?

Motivation comes and goes

Here, it is worth mentioning you don't need to be motivated all the time. Motivation comes and goes. There is no need to beat yourself up when you feel uninspired. To help you take action when you lack motivation it is important to:

- Have a system that allows you to stay on track with your goals

176

- Build the self-discipline needed to do things when you don't feel like it, and
- Have self-compassion and love yourself instead of blaming yourself for everything that goes wrong in your life.

Putting a system in place means having a daily routine that allows you to move toward your goal. For instance, it could be working on a task for a certain amount of time first thing in the morning. Sticking to that ritual every day is one way to build self-discipline. Another way is to set small goals every day and achieve them consistently. Having self-compassion means encouraging yourself instead of beating yourself up.

To learn more about how to create a morning ritual, you can refer to my book, Wake Up Call: How to Take Control of Your Morning and Transform Your Life.

Feeling stuck

Sometimes, you feel stuck. You're not motivated to do anything, or you feel overwhelmed and don't necessarily know why. This often results from either having too many open loops in your life, or from procrastinating on a major task. Let's see what you can do to unstick yourself.

A simple 3-step process to unstick yourself

Whenever you feel stuck try the following 3-step process:

1. Make a list of all the tasks that need to be done.
2. Identify one task you've been putting off.
3. Complete that task.

There is often one specific task you've been putting off for a while.

While this may not necessarily be a difficult task, once you commit and finally complete it, you feel so good you may end up completing many more tasks. As a result, you will start building momentum and allow yourself to get unstuck. If you cannot work on that one specific task, start with a less daunting one. This will also help you build momentum.

Closing open loops

If you've been putting off too many tasks or have too many unfinished projects, you can do the following:

1. Make a list of all the tasks or project you want to complete.
2. Set aside a specific time to complete them. Perhaps, just a few hours could allow you to finish many of these tasks. Or maybe you need longer. If so, take more time.
3. For bigger projects, in the next few days or weeks, focus on only one project until it is complete.
4. Reschedule, delegate or abandon some of your projects.

Action step

Refer to the exercises in the corresponding section of the workbook. (*Section IV. How to use your emotions to grow - Lack of motivation*).

CONCLUSION

Thank you for purchasing this book. My sincere hope is that it helped you make sense of your emotions and gave you the tools you need to start taking better control of them. Remember, the quality of your emotions determines the quality of your life. Therefore, learning how to change yourself and your environment to experience more positive emotions is essential for your wellbeing.

Let's face it. You'll keep experiencing negative emotions throughout your life, but, hopefully, each time you'll remind yourself that your emotions are *not* you and you'll learn to accept them as they are before letting them go. You're *not* sad, depressed, jealous or angry, you are what witnesses these emotions. You are what remains after these temporary feelings fade away.

Your emotions are here to guide you. Learn as much as you can from them, and then let them go. Don't cling to them as if your existence depends on them. It doesn't. Don't identify with them as though they define you. They don't. Instead, use your emotions to grow and remember, you are beyond emotions. How could you not be? They come and go, but you stay. Always.

What do you think?

I want to hear from you! Your thoughts and comments are important to me. If you enjoyed this book or found it useful **I'd be very grateful if you'd post a short review on Amazon.** Your support really does make a difference. I read all the reviews personally so that I can get your feedback and make this book even better.

Thanks again for your support!

Want to listen to the audiobook version for free?

If so, you can use Audible 30-Day Free Trial. To do so:

1. Go to audible.com (or co.uk, fr etc.)
2. Type "Thibaut Meurisse"
3. Click the orange button "Free with 30-day trial" on the right side of the audiobook
4. Get started

Already an audible member?

Look for "Master Your Emotions" on Audible (or iTunes).

Want to master your motivation too?

Master Your Emotions is the first book in the "**Mastery Series**"

You can get the second book, *Master Your Motivation* at the URL below:

http://mybook.to/master_motivation

"In a modern world swamped with information overload, this book is a "best friend" guide to getting you going again whether in business, at home or with life in general."

— AMAZON REVIEWER

"MASTER YOUR MOTIVATION" PREVIEW

Newton's First Law of Motion states that an object in motion stays in motion. This law also applies to human beings—at least in terms of goal setting. In other words, when we are in motion and *actively* moving toward our goals, we can sometimes feel unstoppable. We can experience a state of flow and achieve a lot more than we otherwise would do.

However, what happens when we stop? We might find it hard to start the ball rolling again. As a result, we may end up procrastinating, become depressed or feel frustrated by our lack of action.

Perhaps, this is how you feel now. You may be in one or several of the following situations:

- You feel stuck and lack motivation, unable to make progress on your most important goals.
- You beat yourself up for not getting things done.
- You feel overwhelmed, not knowing what to do next.
- You doubt yourself and worry more than you need to.

- You keep jumping from one task or goal to another, without achieving anything substantial.

If you recognize yourself in any of the above situations, don't worry. This book will help drive you out of your slump and rebuild your motivation.

Fortunately, lacking momentum or feeling stuck is never permanent. You can make it a temporary condition. There are many things you can do to generate motivation and become excited to progress toward your goals and dreams once again.

From time to time, we all feel stuck.

I have moments in my own life when I struggle to complete even the easiest task. In these moments, simply answering one email can become a real challenge. While writing this book, I experienced my fair share of mental blocks, and I had days when I couldn't complete much work. It would be dishonest if I didn't share this truth with you. However, from personal experience, I also know that motivation fluctuates, and that it can return as quickly as it disappeared.

As you apply what you learn in this book, you'll be able to build momentum and generate more consistency in your life. Your motivation will increase and, as a result, you will be able to achieve many more of your goals than you thought possible.

In **Part I** of this book, we'll take a step back and assess your situation from an objective point of view, so you can let go of some of your negative emotions and release the pressure you're piling onto your shoulders.

In **Part II**, we'll see how you can build momentum to help you feel more motivated in your daily life.

In **Part III**, we'll discuss what you can do to sustain that momentum in the long term, to help you maintain a high level of motivation and achieve even more of your goals.

Finally, in **Part IV**, we'll look at the 25 Strategies you can use to rebuild and maintain your motivation.

So, are you ready to boost your motivation and march toward your goals with total confidence?

To get your motivation back today visit the URL below:

mybook.to/master_motivation

Other books by the author:

Crush Your Limits: Break Free From Mental Limitations and Achieve Your True Potential

Goal Setting: The Ultimate Guide to Achieving Goals That Truly Excite You

Habits That Stick: The Ultimate Guide to Building Habits That Stick Once and For All

Master Your Beliefs: A Practical Guide to Stop Doubting Yourself and Build Unshakeable Confidence

Master Your Destiny: A Practical Guide to Rewrite Your Story and Become the Person You Want to Be

Master Your Focus: A Practical Guide to Stop Chasing the Next Thing and Focus on What Matters Until It's Done

Master Your Motivation: A Practical Guide to Unstick Yourself, Build Momentum and Sustain Long-Term Motivation

Master Your Success: Timeless Principles to Develop Inner Confidence and Create Authentic Success

Master Your Thinking: A Practical Guide to Align Yourself wit Reality and Achieve Tangible Results in the Real World

Productivity Beast: An Unconventional Guide to Getting Things Done

Success is Inevitable: 17 Laws to Unlock Your Hidden Potential, Skyrocket Your Confidence and Get What You Want From Life

The Greatness Manifesto: Overcome Your Fear and Go After What You Really Want

The One Goal: Master the Art of Goal Setting, Win Your Inner Battles and Achieve Exceptional Results

The Passion Manifesto: Escape the Rat Race, Uncover Your Passion and Design a Career and Life You Love

The Thriving Introvert: Embrace the Gift of Introversion and Live the Life You Were Meant to Live

The Ultimate Goal Setting Planner: Become an Unstoppable Goal Achiever in 90 Days or Less

Upgrade Yourself: Simple Strategies to Transform Your Mindset, Improve Your Habits and Change Your Life

Wake Up Call: How To Take Control Of Your Morning And Transform Your Life

ABOUT THE AUTHOR

Thibaut Meurisse is a author, coach, and founder of whatispersonaldevelopment.org.

He has been featured on major personal development websites such as Lifehack, TinyBuddha, MotivationGrid, PickTheBrain, DumbLittleMan and FinerMinds.

Obsessed with self-improvement and fascinated by the power of the brain, his personal mission is to help people realize their full potential and reach higher levels of fulfillment and consciousness.

You can connect with him on his Facebook page

https://www.facebook.com/whatispersonaldevelopment.org

Learn more about Thibaut at

amazon.com/author/thibautmeurisse

Bibliography

A Million Thoughts, Learn all about meditation from the Himalayan mystic, Om Swami

Ask and It is Given: Learning to Manifest Your Desires, Esther Hicks and Jerry Hicks

Awareness, Anthony de Mello

Breaking the Chain of Low Self-Esteem, Marilyn Sorensen and Barrie Zwicker

Breathwalk: Breathing Your Way to a Revitalized Body, Mind and Spirit, Gurucharan Singh Khalsa and Yogi Bhajan

Constructive Living, David K. Reynolds

How to Stop Worrying and Start Living, Dale Carnegie

Radical Honesty: How to Transform Your Life by Telling the Truth, Brad Blanton

The Power of Now: A Guide to Spiritual Enlightenment, Eckhart Tolle

The Power of Your Supermind, Vernon Howard

The 15 Commitments of Conscious Leadership: A New Paradigm for Sustainable Success, Jim Dethmer and Diana Chapman

The Sedona Method, Hale Dwoskin and Jack Canfield

The Six Pillars of Self-Esteem, Nathaniel Branden

Step-by-Step
Workbook

PART I. WHAT EMOTIONS ARE

1. Bias towards negativity

Find one example of an imaginary threat resulting from your survival mechanism. Can you see how the mind works? Feel free to write down your example below:

2. Happiness

Identify things that you believe give you shots of dopamine (TV, video games, gambling, social media etc.) . Write them down:

-

-

-

-

Which one of these things are you the most 'addicted' to. What activity, if you were to take a break from, would you be craving? Write it down:

3. The nature of the ego

Write down the things you feel you identify the most with (your body, your relationships, your country, your religion, your car etc.)

-

-

-

-

-

-

-

-

-

-

On a scale of 0 to 10 how true are the following statements?

My ego tends to equate having with being

0 _____ 10

My ego lives through comparison

0 _____ 10

My ego is never satisfied

0 _____ 10

My ego needs other people's approval to feel valued

0 _____ 10

I enhance my value by trying to associate with smart or famous people

0 _____ 10

I like to gossip

0 _____ 10

I have an inferiority complex

0 _____ 10

I have a superiority complex

0 _____ 10

I look for fame

0 _____ 10

I constantly try to be right

0 _____ 10

I often complain

0 _____ 10

I seek attention (recognition, praise or admiration)

0 _____ 10

How does your ego impact your emotion? Write down some of the ways your ego generates negative emotions. Try to be specific.

What could you do about it?

4. The nature of emotions

To help you understand the nature of emotions, we'll focus on just one specific emotion in this section.

Take just a few minutes to go through the following 10 steps by visualizing each step in your mind. If it helps, close your eyes.

Step 1. Select one negative emotion you experienced recently.

My negative emotion:

Step 2. Acknowledge that this emotion isn't bad. See how it comes and goes and isn't you.

Step 3. Remember that emotion and notice how it is nowhere to be found in your present reality.

Step 4. Ask yourself what you can learn from that emotion. What is it trying to tell you and how can you use it to grow?

Step 5. Notice how that negative emotion tainted all your experiences, perhaps, even tricking you to believe you'll never get out it.

Step 6. Remember how you felt the need to identify with this negative emotion and/or with the story that goes with it. Entertain the idea that you could have detached yourself from it.

Step 7. Remember how this negative emotion seemed to narrow down your perspective and limit your potential.

Step 8. See how you were attracting more negative emotions

Step 9. Notice how you created mental suffering out of that emotion by adding your own judgment to it.

Step 10. Finally, realize that your negative emotion exists only in your mind and notice that reality has no problem.

PART II. WHAT IMPACTS YOUR EMOTIONS

You can change your emotions in many different ways. What will you do personally to positively impact your emotions?

1. How will you use your body? What type of exercising will you do? Will you use power posture? (for an example of power posture search for "TED talk Amy Cuddy" on YouTube)

2. How will you use your thoughts? Will you meditate, use positive affirmations or visualization?

Examples:

- I will visualize my goal every morning for 5 minutes allowing myself to feel as if I had already accomplished it
- I will meditate 5 minutes every day for 30 days as soon as I wake up
- I will repeat the affirmation "I love being confident" for 5 minutes every day

3. How will you improve your sleep?

Examples:

- I will meditate before going to bed
- I will create a 10 minutes evening ritual including gratitude exercises, stretching, and meditation

4. How will you use your breathing?

Example: each time I feel some negative emotions, I will breathe slowly for a few minutes

5. How changing your environment could improve your emotions?

Examples:

- I will read inspirational books for 15 minutes each day and cut off the time I spend watching TV
- I will spend less time with negative friends
- I will spend only 15 minutes on social media each day for 30 days

Write down your answers below:

6. How will you use music to improve your mood?

Examples:

- I will listen to gratitude songs while doing my gratitude exercises each morning
- I will listen to/ watch motivational videos when I start feeling a little bit down and dance or move my body to change my emotional state
- I will listen to classical music or white noise to better focus when I work

PART III. HOW TO CHANGE YOUR EMOTIONS

How emotions are formed

Emotions are formed as follows:

- Interpretation + identification + repetition = strong emotion
- Interpretation: When you interpret an event or a thought based on your personal story.
- Identification: When you identify with a specific thought as it arises.
- Repetition: Having the same thoughts over and over.
- Strong emotion: When you experience an emotion so many times that it has become part of your identity. You then experience that emotion whenever a related thoughts or events trigger it.

Revisiting past events

Remember a past event when you experience negative emotions. It could be the last time you were depressed, sad, angry or felt like you weren't good enough.

Now, write down what happens for each of the following:

Interpretation: What events happened and what thoughts arose?

Identification: How did you respond to these thoughts?

Repetition: Did you identify with these thoughts repeatedly?

Changing your story

Analyze your story by answering the questions below:

One or two emotional issues you currently have. Ask yourself, "What emotions if I could get rid of, would have the most positive impact on my life?"

Your interpretation of these issues. Ask yourself, "What would I need to believe for my story to be true?"

New empowering meanings that will help you deal with these issues. Ask yourself, "What would I need to believe to avoid experiencing these negative emotions?"

Letting go of your emotions

Make a list of the emotions you would like to let go of.

Perhaps, you feel like you aren't good enough. Or you struggle with procrastination. Or maybe you blame yourself for something you did in the past. Just write down whatever comes to your mind.

-

-

-

-

-

-

-

Select one emotion then ask yourself:

"Could I let this feeling go?"

"Would I"? (Yes/no)

"When?" (NOW)

The emotion I want to let go of:

Additional tip:

Keep practicing letting go of emotions in your day-to-day life

Conditioning your mind

Get into the habit of depositing positive thoughts in your mind every day. Choose one emotion you want to experience more of in your life and commit to conditioning your mind every day for at least 30 days.

Examples of emotions:

- Gratitude
- Excitement
- Self-esteem
- Certainty
- Decisiveness

My emotion(s):

How exactly I will condition my mind:

Example: I will close my eyes and say "thank you" to all people that cross my mind while acknowledging one good thing they did for me.

Changing your emotions by changing your behaviors

Remember the last time you experience a negative emotion that lasted for a couple of days or more. Write it down below:

Now, write down what you did specifically to overcome that negative emotion:

Then, ask yourself, "How could I have changed my behavior in such a way that it would have influenced my emotions positively?". Write it down below:

Changing your environment

Write down below any activities that you believe may negatively impact your emotions.

Examples: Negative friends, TV, gossiping, social media, video games etc.

-

-

-

-

-

-

Next to each activity write down what are the consequences (It makes you feel guilty, demotivates you, erodes your self-esteem etc.)

Write down what you could instead that you improve your mood

-

-

-

-

-

PART IV. HOW TO USE YOUR EMOTIONS TO GROW

Record your emotions

Spend a couple of minutes each day to record how you feel and rate yourself on a scale of 1 to 10, one being the worse you could feel and ten being the best. At the end of the week, give yourself an overall note and answer the following questions:

What negative emotions did you experience?

What caused these emotions? (Did specific thoughts/external events lead you to feel the way?)

What really happened?

What was your interpretation of what happened?

What would you need to believe to feel that way?

Are your beliefs true?

If you had interpreted thoughts or events differently, could you have felt better?

How did you get back to your neutral state?

What happened exactly? (Did you change your thoughts, take action or did it happen naturally?)

What could you have done to avoid or reduce these negative emotions?

Not being good enough

Identify triggers

What thought are you identifying with? Which areas of your life are concerned?

Write down the following:

Situations in which you feel like you aren't good enough

-

-

-

-

-

-

-

Thoughts you identify with (your story)

-

-

-

-

-

-

Overcoming the feeling of unworthiness

Keeping track of your accomplishments

Exercise 1 - Create a win log

Write down your daily accomplishments. For this exercise, I encourage you to use a dedicated notebook.

- Write down all the things you've accomplished in your life. Come up with a list of fifty things.
- At the end of each day, write down all the things you've accomplished that day.

Try to come up with 5 to 10 things each day.

Exercise 2 - Fill up your self-esteem jar

write down each thing you've accomplished on separate pieces of paper and put them into a jar.

Exercise 3 - Create a positive journal

Write down every compliment you receive. Your colleague told you your shoes look nice, write it down. Your friend complimented your hair, write it down. Your boss told you you did a great job, write it down as well.

Learn to accept compliments

Exercise 1 - Accept compliments

This simple exercise is here to help you accept a compliment. Whenever someone compliments you, say the following:

Thank you *insert the person's name*.

No "Thank you, but...", "Thank you, you too" or "It wasn't a big deal", just "Thank you".

Exercise 2 - Appreciation game

The purpose of this game is to learn to appreciate things about yourself than you didn't previously acknowledge (or like). Tell your partner three things you appreciate about them and ask them to do the same. Be as specific as possible and don't worry about coming up with big things.

Below are some examples:

- I appreciate that you prepared breakfast this morning even though you were in a rush
- I appreciate that you picked up the kids today
- I appreciate the way you always listen to my problems after work

Getting defensive

Whenever you get defensive, ask yourself the following questions:

- What am I trying to protect here?
- Can I let go of that belief?
- What would I be without that belief?

Stress/Worry

Make a list of your major sources of stress

Write down what causes the most stress in your typical week. Come up with at least ten things.

-

-

-

-

-

-

-

-

-

-

-

Reframe the situation

Now, for each thing ask yourself the following questions:

- Is that situation stressful in itself?
- What would I need to believe in order to experience stress in that specific situation?
- What would I need to believe in order to reduce/remove stress in that particular situation?

Make a list of your worries

As you did with stressful situations, make a list of things (past or future) you worry about. You may end up writing similar things as in the previous examples and that's fine.

Examples of things you may worry about are your health, your financial situation, your work, your relationships or your family

Now, write at least ten things you're worrying about in a typical week.

-

-

-

-

-

-

-

-

-

-

-

Sort out your worries

- Look at your list of stressful situations. Next to each item put a C (control), a SM (Some control) or an NC (No control).
- Now, for things you have (some) control over, write down what you could do about it. What concrete actions could you take?

Change, reframe or eliminate stressful situations

Go over your list and look for things you have no control over. Write down below what you could do to change, reframe or eliminate these things. If you can't do anything, can you let go of your need to control them and, instead, accept them?

Caring what people think of you

Change your view of the way people perceive you

Exercise 1 - Realizing people don't care

This exercise will help you understand at a deeper level that most people are not really concerned about you.

Write down the name of one person you know:

Write down how often you're thinking about that person in your day-to-day life:

Now, put yourself in the shoes of that person. How much do you think he or she thinks about you?

How much is he or she taking notes of what you do or say?

What do you think he or she is worrying about right now?

Repeat this process with at least two more people

Exercise 2 - Realizing that you do not care

- Go through your day and try to remember all the people you met or interacted with. It might the waitress in the restaurant you went to for lunch, people you saw on the street etc.
- Now ask yourself how much you thought about these people prior to this exercise.
- Acknowledge the fact you don't think of other people much and neither do they. Let it sink and allow yourself to feel liberated

Stop being overly attached to your self-image

Write down below all the things you're afraid to be judged on. Maybe you worry about your look or you're afraid of saying something silly:

-

-

-

-

-

-

For each item on your list write down why you care. What is the issue here? What image are you trying to protect?

-

-

-

-

-

-

Resentment

4-step method to let go of resentment

1. Changing/reevaluating your interpretation

Write down what exactly happened. After you remove your interpretation, what are the hard facts?

2. Confronting the situation

If your resentment is directed toward people, perhaps, you need to have an honest discussion with them. If you can't talk to that person directly, you can write a letter. Even if you don't send it, the simple act of writing a letter may help you let go of some of your resentment.

3. Forgiving

Now, that you've found a channel to express yourself, you can forgive. Write down how your resentment affects your happiness and peace of mind:

Now, imagine how your life would be and how you would feel once you let go of resentment. Do it right now. Let go and allow yourself to forgive.

4. Forgetting

Finally, forget. Commit to letting go of thoughts of resentment. When such thoughts arise, let go of them.

Depression

Reconnect with your body and your emotions

Do one or several of the following things:

- **Exercise:** Exercising is a great way to calm your mind and connect with your body and has a positive effect on your mood.
- **Meditate:** Meditation is a great way to observe your mind and stop identifying with your thoughts so heavily.
- **Get busy:** Getting busy allows you to avoid excessive thinking.
- **Focus on other:** Dale Carnegie in his book How to Stop Worrying and Start Living, argues that depression can be cured in 14 days. How? Just by thinking of ways to help one person every day for two weeks.

Jealousy

Identify who you are jealous of

Write down who you are jealous of. Now, what does it say about you and what you want from life?

Cooperate rather than compete

Think of a time in the past when you felt jealous of someone else's accomplishments. Now, ask yourself why you felt that way. Then, ask yourself:

- What would supporting that person look like?
- How could I cooperate with the person?
- Why is that person's success good for me?

Compare apples to apples

Select someone you often compare yourself to. Write down all the things you're doing better than that person

Things I'm doing better:

-

-

-

-

-

-

Then, acknowledge how biased your initial comparison was.

Fear/Discomfort

Move out of your comfort zone

- "What is the one thing that I know I should be doing, but that I have procrastinated on because of fear?". Do that thing.
- Every day do one thing that make you uncomfortable (even just a little bit)

Procrastination

How to Crush Procrastination in 16 Simple Steps

1. Understand what's hidden behind procrastination.

Make sure you identify all the reasons behind procrastination and be honest with yourself. If you lack motivation, ask yourself why.

2. Remind yourself of the cost of procrastination

Procrastination is not a minor issue. Its cost is both direct and indirect:

- The direct consequence of procrastination is that you'll achieve far less than you could during your time spent on earth.
- The indirect consequence of procrastination is that you may feel bad about yourself.

Write down what procrastination costs you. How does it affect your peace of mind? Your self-esteem? Your ability to achieve your dreams?

-

-

-

-

-

3. Uncover your story

Write down all your excuses. Then, address them one by one. (examples: I don't have time, I'm too old, I'm not smart enough, I'm too tired etc.)

-

-

-

-

-

-

4. Rewrite your story

Look at your excuses. Now that you've identified your story, create a new more empowering story to neutralize your old excuses. See examples below:

- I don't have time for that → I find and make time for whatever I'm committed to.
- I'm too tired → I have control over my mind and I have

more energy than I think. When I schedule a task I complete it.

Create affirmations or mantras around your new story. Repeat them to yourself every morning and throughout the day until they become part of your identity.

Your affirmation(s):

5. Clarify your why

Look at one important task you regularly procrastinate on. Why is that? Write down how you can make these tasks part of your vision:

6. Identify the ways you distract yourself

What are your own ways to procrastinate on that important task?

Examples: going for a walk, watching videos on Youtube, checking Facebook etc.

How I procrastinate:

7. Stay with the urge

As you feel the urge to *insert your distraction here*, stay with the emotion. How do you feel? Allow yourself to feel that emotion. Don't judge yourself. Don't blame yourself. Just accept what is. As you do so, you'll gain more control of your mind.

8. Record everything you do

Record everything you do for a week. Then, see how much time you spend doing unproductive activities.

9. Set a clear intent behind everything you do

Before working on a task, make sure you know exactly what needs to be done. Ask yourself, what am I trying to accomplish here?

10. Prepare your environment

Your mind doesn't like what's hard. It wants things to be easy. Thus, make sure you can start working on your task immediately by removing any friction or obstacle.

Write down below what you can do to make it easier to work on your important task:

11. Start small

Making your tasks smaller will help you overcome procrastination. Not only that, but it will also allow you to build momentum.

Chunk down your important task:

12. Create quick wins

Set small goals every day and accomplish them consistently for a few weeks. As you do that you'll increase your self-esteem and be better equipped to complete more challenging tasks in the future.

Write quick wins for your task(s) (select 1 to 3 tasks)

-

-

-

13. Just get started

Often, when you start working on a task, you'll enter what is called 'the flow' and things become effortless. Look at the quick wins you wrote down previously and take a few seconds to commit to getting started on these tasks.

14. Create daily habits to support you

If you tend to procrastinate on important tasks, commit to working on them first thing in the morning. Write down one task you will work on first thing in the morning.

My one task:

15. Use visualization

You can also use visualization to help you overcome procrastination. Below are two specific ways you can do so:

1. Visualizing yourself doing the task: Before you start a task, visualize yourself working on it.

2. Visualizing yourself having completed the task: Imagine yourself having completed the task. How would you feel once the task is done? Liberated? Happy? Proud?

Additional tip:

Each time you finish a challenging task, take a few seconds to notice how that makes you feel. Remind yourself of that feeling whenever you start working on a difficult task.

16. Build accountability

How can you build accountability for your important tasks and goals (examples: have an accountability partner, hire a coach, send your list of goals to a friend every week etc.)

Lack of motivation

Creating a system

To help you take action when you lack motivation it is important to:

- Have a system that allows you to stay on track with your goals
- Build the self-discipline needed to do things when you don't feel like it
- Have self-compassion and love yourself instead of blaming yourself

What daily routine can you put in place to stay on track with your goals? (examples: create a morning ritual with positive affirmations, visualizations or work on your most important task first thing in the morning)

To build self-discipline, what task can you commit to doing every day for the next 30 days?

My tasks:

What words of encouragement or mantras can you use to encourage yourself when you feel down?